Not Your Mother's Slow Cooker Recipes for Two

Also by Beth Hensperger

The Gourmet Potluck

The Bread Lover's Bread Machine Cookbook

The Best Quick Breads

Bread for Breakfast

Bread Made Easy

The Pleasure of Whole Grain Breads

The Bread Bible

Breads of the Southwest

Beth's Basic Bread Book

Bread for all Seasons

Baking Bread

Bread

By Beth Hensperger and Julie Kaufmann

Not Your Mother's Slow Cooker Cookbook

The Ultimate Rice Cooker Cookbook

Not Your Mother's Slow Cooker Recipes for Two

Beth Hensperger

The Harvard Common Press
Boston, Massachusetts

THE HARVARD COMMON PRESS
535 Albany Street
Boston, Massachusetts 02118
www.harvardcommonpress.com

Printed in the United States of America
Printed on acid-free paper

Library of Congress Cataloging-in-Publication Data
   Hensperger, Beth
     Not your mother's slow cooker recipes for two / Beth Hensperger.
        p.   cm.
     Includes index.
     ISBN 1-55832-341-4 (pbk. : alk. paper) — ISBN 1-55832-340-6 (hardcover : alk. paper)
        1. Electric cookery, Slow. 2. Cookery for two. I. Title. II. Title: Recipes for two.
     TX827.H392   2007
     641.5'612dc222   2006016735

ISBN-13: 978-1-55832-340-7 (hardcover); 978-1-55832-341-4 (paperback)
ISBN-10: 1-55832-340-6 (hardcover); 1-55832-341-4 (paperback)

Special bulk-order discounts are available on this and other Harvard Common Press books.
Companies and organizations may purchase books for premiums or resale, or may arrange
a custom edition, by contacting the Marketing Director at the address above.

Book design by rlf design
Cover photography by Eskite Photography

10 9 8 7 6 5 4 3

Thank you to Bruce Shaw,
founder and publisher of
The Harvard Common Press,
for his vision of the original book idea
and his full support throughout
the writing of my slow cooker cookbooks

Acknowledgments

With pleasure and joy, I acknowledge the following people who were so helpful with their contributions to this book: Lynn Alley, Martha Casselman, Jesse Cool, Mary Ellen Evans, Peggy Fallon, Joyce Goldstein, Lou Pappas, Nancyjo Riekse, Little Ricky Rodgers, Meg and Don Rohacek, and Judith Thomas.

Special thanks go to Bobbe and Bill Torgerson for their creativity, patience, and expert advice. Thank you to executive editor Valerie Cimino for her time and extraordinary energy in making this book the best it could be.

Thank you to Kathy Benson, director of marketing services at West Bend Housewares; Susan Jones, marketing director at Hamilton Beach/Proctor-Silex, Inc.; and Yvonne Olson, slow cooker product manager at Hamilton Beach/Proctor-Silex, Inc., for providing support on this project by contributing the baby slow cookers with interest and enthusiasm.

Warm, sincere thanks to everyone!

Contents

Introduction

In the 1950s, my parents used to watch a TV show called the *Loretta Young Theatre*, starring, of course, the famous movie actress Loretta Young. One of the segments featured the star cooking different meals while daydreaming. Loretta prepared her meals with the saddest face, since she was alone, and cooked from an open book to the side of the small stove. The name of the cookbook was *Cooking for One Can Be Fun*. Of course, the gist of the story was that cooking for her was not fun.

Our society has come a long way since then. No longer is the large family the norm. There are many singles and couples, and they all want to feed themselves well. Statistics back this up, with at present one-third of American families containing two people. After the publication of *Not Your Mother's Slow Cooker Cookbook* (The Harvard Common Press, 2005), I was deluged with requests for a collection of scaled-down slow cooker recipes designed for one or two people.

The larger-capacity slow cookers, which slow cooker recipes are most often geared for, are just too big for smaller-quantity cooking. Since there is a recommended volume for each cooker for optimum efficiency, using a smaller amount of food in the larger cooker means that the food does not cook as well as the machine is designed to do. The smaller cookers, with a 1½- to 3-quart capacity, fill this need perfectly, and there are new varieties of these smaller cookers emerging, as attractive as they are utilitarian, so that you can now choose from a round or oval shape, multiple heat settings, and a variety of styles.

Even though I am cooking for myself, or myself and one other person, I want the food I eat to be imaginative, plentiful, and varied, based on easily obtainable seasonal ingredients. It is interesting to note that, according to research, most people who cook for themselves use and rotate, at most, only a dozen or so recipes. Although these recipes may vary in ingredients from time to time, they remain the core of most meals prepared. Thus, everyday meals can become so routine that any mealtime excitement is lost. The collection of recipes in this book is designed to expand and enhance your existing repertoire of dishes, and I hope that you will enjoy the new variety you will find in these pages.

I am a proponent of wholesome, fresh food, and the slow cooker fits into not only my food philosophy but my time schedule as well. I offer here a wide range of recipes focusing on meat, poultry, and beans in one-pot main-dish stews, braises, and soups. Some of the dishes are my adapta-tions of classic combinations, recipes that are permanently a part of the diet of most Americans, and others are my own invention or contemporary twists on traditional recipes—recipes that reflect the growing interest in light, healthy fare. They have the following taste and technique attributes in common: They are extremely practical, they are simple to assemble and prep, and they cook in the unrushed and unattended style we have come to expect from slow cooker cuisine. They take advantage of wholesome and healthful basic ingredients, a trademark of all my cookbooks.

Whether I am out of the house all day or working at home, cooking for myself or for a guest, the convenience offered by the slow cooker style of cooking is remarkable. The food from this humble, inexpensive countertop appliance turns out rich, savory, and satisfying. All the recipes in this book are as suitable for eating alone or in a duo on a busy weeknight as they are for a weekend dinner or a no-fuss holiday meal. There is often enough left over for a second meal, to be refrigerated or frozen and eaten another time. I want the cook, despite any time limitations or even a lag in interest for food preparation, to be relaxed and confident while the flavors develop in the pot, and then to be beautifully fed. Happy slow cooking!

A New Take on Slow and Savory

What is slow cooker cooking? All foods are cooked by one of two heat methods: moist or dry. Dry-heat cooking methods include roasting, baking, broiling, grilling, toasting, pan-frying, and deep frying. This method uses appliances like microwaves, toasters, and conventional ovens. Moist-heat cooking includes stewing, braising, steaming, and poaching, and uses appliances such as microwaves, ovens, and stovetops.

The slow cooker, with its even, low heat in a covered pot, is the master of the moist-heat technique, most specifically braising, to cook food. Slow cookers single-handedly have brought braised food, although always a preferred method of family-style cooking, back into the realm of day-to-day cooking. Recipes that were once reserved for large-quantity cooking or for company only are now no more complex than braising a simple chicken breast or lamb chop. In short, because of the slow cooker, braising for two is now as easy as cooking for a crowd.

Moist-heat cooking involves cooking meat and other foods in a constantly moving environment of liquid or steam. It is used for foods that are not naturally tender, such as meat with a lot of connective tissue and plants with lots of fiber, such as beans. It is the most efficient way to transform tough meat into delectably tender morsels.

Braising is an excellent way of cooking inexpensive cuts of meat—the flavors heighten and the liquid literally cooks the meat. Braises and stews are creative in that cooks can achieve infinite variety by varying the liquid (such as water, stock, wine, or juice) and by using a combination of two cooking techniques. "Braising" comes from the French word *braise*, which translates to "ember," giving testament to its long use by humans to cook food. Its counterpart is stewing, where the meat is cut into uniform small pieces that are almost submerged; the cooking liquid becomes the sauce. Both techniques call for a deep, thick earthenware cooking pot for optimum efficiency, yet it should be small enough so the meat fits snugly and have a tight lid to retain the cooking steam. While stews may have an image problem—appearing so humble that they are often overlooked by cooks who are more impressed with stylish plated food—there is nothing as satisfying or fragrant as a well-made country-style stew.

While dry-heat cooking circulates hot dry air, moist-heat cooking is a far more efficient method of cooking, since food reaches a temperature that is the same on the surface of the food as it is in the interior. Moist heat reaches a proper cooking temperature quickly and maintains it more consistently; since water heats only to its boiling point of 212°F, foods do not burn and can handle long cooking times without being monitored (in dry-heat cooking, the higher heat is what browns the surface). This style of cooking is known for its ease, economy, tenderness, and flavor. The different types of moist-heat techniques differ from one another in the amount of liquid used. Braising and steaming take a modicum of liquid, stews a bit more, and poaching fully submerges the food.

How Does a Slow Cooker Work?

Today's new machines are a great improvement over those on the market even five years ago, and since they are such an inexpensive appliance, go ahead and upgrade from your mom's hand-me-down or that one you picked up at a tag sale. If you cook a lot, buy a second or third machine in a different size (you won't regret doing so).

The slow cooker's low-wattage, wrap-around heating coils are sandwiched between inner and outer metal walls for indirect heat; the heat source never makes direct contact with the stoneware crock. The coils inside the walls heat up, and the space between the base wall and the crock heats up, transferring that heat to the stoneware insert. The slow cooker cooks at a temperature between 200° and 300°F.

In this book, I never indicate a specific cooking temperature in a recipe, because the cooking process is based on the wattage of the slow cooker and time. The contents of the crock will take 1 to 2 hours to heat up to a simmer, much slower than in any other cooking process, so relax and be prepared for this. Many cooks turn the cooker to the HIGH heat setting for 1 to 2 hours to bring the temperature up as quickly as possible to 140°F, the temperature at which bacteria can no longer proliferate in food, then switch to LOW for the remainder of the cook time. Any time you lift the lid to check the contents or to stir, you release the accumulated steam that cooks the food, and it will take approximately 20 minutes for the internal cook temperature to come back to the stable cooking temperature. Therefore, while you are cooking, do not open the lid repeatedly to examine the contents. The accumulated steam is part of the cooking process (you'll know that the machine is doing its job properly when you cannot see through the clear lid into the pot due to its steaming up), although it is hard not to keep checking the first time you use a slow cooker. But remember that opening the lid more than a couple of times slows down the cooking considerably.

During cooking, the outside of the cooker's metal base housing will become hot to the touch, so keep it away from children and walls or low cabinets. The stoneware insert will slowly reach the same high temperature, although you can briefly touch both without oven mitts to check the temperature. If you are transferring the whole dish to a buffet or potluck dinner, just carry the entire portable unit by its handles, then plug it in and set the heat to LOW to reheat the food. There are optional accessories for transporting the slow cooker, such as a Lid Latch from Rival, which keeps the lid in place while you carry the cooker, and a lovely insulated carrying case.

What Is the Best Size Slow Cooker for Cooking Solo and for Two?

This book is specifically geared toward preparing recipes that are suited to the small-capacity slow cooker countertop appliance. The slow cooker has been marketed in past decades as appealing to the needs of larger families and to anyone who needs large quantities of food. *Not Your Mother's Slow Cooker Recipes for Two* is establishing new territory by addressing the needs of singles and couples who also wish to take advantage of the convenience and delicious food that is available from the slow cooker method of cooking.

First, here is the overall view. The slow cooker is available in a wide range of volume capacities from 1 quart to 7 quarts, in 2-cup increments. The sizes are divided into three general categories: small (1½-, 2-, 2½-, and 3-quart capacity), medium (3½-, 4-, and 4½-quart capacity), and large (5-, 5½-, 6-, and 7-quart capacity). Almost all sizes come in a choice of round or oval, but be sure to check inside the box and on the carton label when purchasing, as often the picture on the outside of the box is not the shape of the cooker within. If you have a choice, always choose the oval shape. It is a bit more compact than the round and has more cooking surface area, easily fitting a turkey breast or two chops side by side.

What is smaller-quantity slow cooking? It is cooking a meal for one or two people, often, but not always, with leftovers, depending on your needs. The most efficient machine for this quantity is the small cooker (specifically a 1½-, 2-, 2½-, or 3-quart machine). It is an attractive and easy-to-manipulate appliance, since it is not as cumbersome or heavy as the larger crocks. It is comfortable to lift, fits nicely on the counter and does not take up much space, and the crockery insert can even fit on the top rack in the dishwasher. You do not want the smallest machine, the 16-ounce size, dubbed the Little Dipper by Rival. This size is great for keeping dips warm on a buffet table or for melting chocolate, but it is not the size you want to use for daily meals. It is too small for cooking soups, stews, and various cuts of meat.

While small cookers used to be designed without removable crocks and only came

---

·· Manufacturers of Small Slow Cookers ··

1½- and 3-quart oval, 1½-quart round

Proctor-Silex Slow Cookers
800-851-8900
www.proctorsilex.com

1½- and 2½-quart round, 3- and 3½-quart oval

Rival Crock-Pots
800-557-4825
www.crockpot.com

Rival offers numerous models in round or oval shapes, though all of their small machines are round. You can order accessories via their Web site, such as bake pans, meat racks, disposable bag liners for the crockery insert, vinyl storage covers, and insulated travel bags.

3-quart oval

West Bend Housewares Crockery Cookers
262-334-6949
www.westbend.com

The 3-quart is the smallest size they make. It has a great nonstick interior.

---

in the round shape with an ON/OFF function controlled by pulling the plug in and out of the socket, these older cookers will not work best for the recipes in this book. You definitely want a machine with multiple heat settings, preferably with KEEP WARM, LOW, and HIGH settings. For solo cooking I love the 1½-quart oval, but many slow cooker users who cook for one or two people use a 2½- to 3½-quart model, because they want the versatility to be able to cook for guests or have leftovers. Hard-core slow cooker users usually have two or three machines in different sizes, and once you get started cooking, you'll understand why. I have both 1½- and 3-quart oval cookers from Proctor-Silex, with which I tested all the recipes in this book. I also tested recipes using machines from Rival and West Bend.

The 3-quart oval became a very popular model with me and co-author Julie Kaufmann during the testing of the recipes in *Not Your Mother's Slow Cooker Cookbook*. For your first foray into slow cooking, this is the size I recommend. It holds 4 servings of stew, a 3-pound roast, or a cut-up whole chicken. This is also a good size for two people who like leftovers, which can be reheated within a few days or frozen for a later meal. Many people use the 3-quart oval to cook for one person, especially for stews, soups, and chili.

So, when introduced to the 1½-quart oval and the 2½-quart round cookers, I was not prepared for my reaction: I fell in love with the sizes and wanted to make slow-cooked meals every day. I quickly augmented my 3-quart oval with these smaller sizes. The 1½-quart oval is a boon for the single cook. I do not recommend you use a round cooker in this size; the oval gives so much more possibility to your cooking—it can cook two pork chops, one large osso buco, or boneless chicken breasts side by side. You can cook a whole pork tenderloin in it and make a myriad of soups and stews. You can cook for yourself, yet have enough for another meal or to share with a guest.

How to Use a Slow Cooker for the First Time

While the slow cooker is very simple to use, there is a sequence of use. There are no moving parts, so your slow cooker is delightfully uncomplicated. When shopping for a slow cooker, do check inside the box before purchasing to make sure that all parts are intact and that its shape, which may be different from what is pictured on the outside of the box, is what you intended to buy.

Read the manufacturer's booklet, highlighting warranty information and customer service phone numbers, and fill out the warranty card. Make a note in the back of the booklet regarding the model and capacity—a note that is especially useful as time goes by and you forget what size your crock is. Then familiarize yourself with my Slow Cooker Tips for Success (see page 7).

I recommend that you stay in the house during your first use of this appliance to assess how it works and observe the cooking process. Slow cookers do not have a thermostat, so if you are concerned about temperature, use a dial food thermometer inserted into the meat or cooking liquid.

1. Place the cooker on your countertop. Place the machine away from the wall and sink and close to an electrical outlet, since the cord is quite short. *Do not* use an extension cord or plug strip.

2. Remove the lid and stoneware insert and wash them in hot, soapy water, taking care not to scratch them; both the lid and the stoneware are dishwasher safe. Dry the stoneware thoroughly and place it back into the base by sliding it into place. If it is a round machine, line up the handles on the insert and base. Put on the lid and leave it on the counter until you are ready to cook.

3. After choosing a recipe, read the recipe carefully through to the end before starting to cook to be sure you have all the ingredients and can make any adjustments, know the procedures, assemble the utensils and other appliances, and know how long the cooking time will be. *Then* chop, mince, shred, dice, cut, grate, and do any other food prep required. If you cut up your meat and vegetables in advance, store them separately, covered, in the refrigerator. I prefer to remove the stoneware and fill it outside the base so as not to

splash liquid into the base. In general to avoid spillage, do not fill the crock more than three-quarters full, as the heated contents will expand. Also note that the heating coils do not go all the way to the top. Carefully replace the crock into the base, wipe the edges clean, then cover with the lid. Plug in.

4. Set the machine to the ON, LOW, or HIGH heat setting, as directed in the recipe. Some simpler, usually smaller, machines do not have a switch; they are turned on whenever they are plugged in, and you must unplug them to turn them off. Do not ever cook on the KEEP WARM setting, even if you think the LOW setting is cooking at too high a temperature.

5. Set a timer or write down the estimated cooking time as per the recipe instructions. It is best to check the food at the first time suggestion or a bit earlier, especially when making a recipe for the first time. Use a wooden or heat-resistant spoon or spatula to stir or serve (metal utensils, spoons, and whisks are fine as long as you are careful not to chip the crock). If using an immersion blender to puree soups, be sure to keep it from hitting the sides of the crock, and unplug the unit first.

6. When handling the full stoneware crock, always turn off the machine and unplug it first, then use thick

oven mitts to transfer the hot crock to a hot pad or heatproof surface. You can serve directly out of the crock, either in or out of its base. At the end of the cook time, you can leave the full crock in the housing base until it is cool enough to handle to transfer the contents to a refrigerator container. Do not ever fill the hot stoneware with cold water to soak; you could crack it. Once the crock has cooled, you can use it to store leftovers in the refrigerator.

Slow Cooker Tips for Success

There is a saying that what appears to be easy often is not, and the impression of effortlessness is usually the result of much unseen effort. This is an apt description of bistro-style braising, with its earthy honesty and time-honored methods that go back to home hearth cooking. But the slow cooker has made this axiom true—what looks easy *is* easy, and the effort expended is quite often minimal for the results, which rival arduous and great country-style cooking. Once you become familiar with the new techniques involved with using your slow cooker, you will probably wonder how you ever did without it as an essential kitchen appliance. Once I got past the idea of the "magic pot" (that is, that you randomly throw in some raw ingredients and they are magically transformed into a fabulous meal) and began using the slow cooker in various practical

capacities, I gained a new respect for this trendsetting appliance.

Please be sure to read this section before your first slow cooking forays and use it as a reference guide thereafter, as the slow cooker requires that you follow some very important guidelines for safe cooking.

- Unless you are cooking at the wrong temperature, have used too much or too little liquid, have let a dish cook too long, or have overfilled the crockery insert, there will be no burning, sticking, or bubbling over. Exceptions might occur in recipes that specify to cook on HIGH heat with the cover off to encourage evaporation of liquid.

- Never preheat an empty crockery insert before adding the food. Load the crock with the ingredients and then turn on the heat or plug in to start the heating process.

- The cord on the slow cooker is deliberately short to minimize danger from tangling or tripping. You may use a heavy-duty extension cord *only* if it has a marked electrical rating at least as great as the electrical rating of your cooker, but I advise against using an extension cord, to minimize risk of overturning the pot.

- For food safety considerations, most slow cooker appliances do not allow you to pre-program the cooking start time. That means you cannot fill the pot with food, leave home, and have the pot go on an hour or two later. While food is cooking and once it's done, food will stay safe for as long as the cooker is operating. The newer programmable machines have strict food safety guidelines accompanying the appliance. At this writing, this feature is only available on the large machines.

- When beginning to cook or to hasten the cooking process, switch from the LOW to the HIGH heat setting. In general, the cooking time on HIGH is about half of the cooking time on LOW. One hour on HIGH is 2 to 2½ hours on LOW. These recipes specify the best temperature setting for each recipe to achieve the best results. We have found that the new slow cookers are much more efficient and run at slightly higher temperatures than do older cookers. Be sure to check the wattage of your unit; there are slight differences between manufacturers. Some recipes turn out better on LOW with a gentle rolling simmer than with the vigorous simmer on HIGH. Many cooks always start their cookers on HIGH for about an hour to get a good start on the cooking, then switch to LOW.

- The glass lid becomes quite hot during the cooking process. Use a potholder to remove it if necessary, and handle it with care to avoid burns. Keeping the lid in place during cooking is essential for proper cooking of the contents of the crock. The lid is dishwasher-safe.

- The amount of liquid used varies drastically in the recipes, from a few tablespoons to cover the bottom of the crock to submerging the food completely in liquid. Each recipe will be specific on these points. Fill the cooker with the solid ingredients, place in the base, and then carefully add the liquid, to avoid both splashing and having to lift an overly heavy crock.

- Ideally, slow cooker crockery inserts should be filled from half full to no more than 1 inch from the rim. The best practice is to fill the insert one-half to three-quarters full, because the heating elements are around the sides of the insert; this will give you the most even cooking and will help avoid spills as the heated contents expand. Root vegetables cook more slowly than meat and poultry in a slow cooker, so if you are using them, place the vegetables in first, at the bottom and around the sides of the cooking vessel, in a layered effect. Then add meat and cover the food with liquid such as broth, water, or tomato or barbecue sauce.

- Check the food for doneness once toward the middle of the cook time, then again around the time suggested in the recipe for the minimum amount of cooking, especially the first time you make a dish.

- Tender vegetables and pasta overcook easily, so add them during the last 30 to 60 minutes of cooking. The same goes for cooking with any seafood. For the most control over seasoning, add that during the last hour as well. While dried herbs and spices do work nicely when added at the beginning with the bulk of the ingredients, remember that their flavors will concentrate, so do not add too much; you can always add more at the end of cooking. Fresh herbs are best added at the end, as they tend to break down and dissolve if added in the beginning. Salt and pepper can be added at any point in the cooking process, except when you are cooking legumes or stock; then salt should not be added until the end.

o While the crockery insert can be used in a conventional oven, it cannot be used on a gas or electric stovetop; it will break in direct contact with a heating element, as will any ceramic dish. If browning ingredients, such as searing meat, do so first in a sauté pan, skillet, or saucepan, as directed in the recipe, then transfer into the crock. The manufacturer's directions will specify if the crock is ovenproof, microwave-safe, or broiler-safe.

o At the end of the cooking time, remove the lid and stir well, preferably with a wooden or heatproof plastic spoon to prevent chipping the crock. If your dish is not cooked to your preference at the end of the designated cooking time, replace the lid, set the temperature to HIGH, and cook in additional increments of 30 to 60 minutes until the food is done. Don't worry if the dish takes longer than the recipe says; there are many variables among machines and in the temperature of the

ingredients that can affect the cooking time.

o When the food is cooked and ready to be served, turn the cooker to the OFF setting and/or unplug the unit. Many older slow cookers and small units do not have an OFF setting; "off" is when the unit is unplugged. The stoneware crock will retain heat, keeping food warm, for a full hour after turning off the machine.

o Once the dish is completely cooked, you can keep the food hot by switching to the LOW or KEEP WARM setting. Food can be held safely in the cooker for up to 2 hours before eating. Many digital cookers switch automatically to the KEEP WARM setting when the cooking time is up. Do not use the KEEP WARM setting, if you have one, for cooking; the temperature is too low.

o The crock will be very hot at the end of cooking, so if not serving directly out of the cooker, use heavy oven mitts to lift the hot crock with its contents carefully out of the base. Transfer to a skid-proof trivet or folded towel.

o Transfer leftovers to proper refrigerator or freezer storage containers within two hours after finishing cooking. Do not refrigerate your hot cooked food in the crockery insert, as the insert may crack.

o Ceramic clay cookware cannot withstand quick changes in temperature. Never store the stoneware crock in the freezer. The insert can also crack if you add a lot of frozen food or submerge it in cold water while it is still hot from the cooking cycle. Be sure to let the crock come to room temperature before washing; never pour cold water into a hot crock. If your insert becomes cracked or deeply scratched, contact the manufacturer for replacement instructions. The crock can be washed by hand with nonabrasive dish soap and a nylon scrub pad, or placed in the dishwasher.

○ Cold cooked food should not be reheated in the crockery insert, as it will take too long to reach an internal temperature that renders the food safe to eat. However, cooked food can be brought to steaming on the stove or in a microwave and then put into a slow cooker crock on the LOW or KEEP WARM setting to keep hot for serving.

○ Never immerse the metal housing base of the slow cooker in water or fill it with liquids for cooking; you must always have the crockery insert in place to cook. To clean the base, let it come to room temperature or fill with the hottest tap water possible, then wipe the inside and outside with a

·· Cooking Time Conversion Chart ··

Use this indispensable conversion chart as a guide for translating traditional cooking times to slow cooker times. All times are approximate, and, when making a recipe for the first time, be sure to make notes on the cooking time for further reference. While early slow cooker recipes designated both LOW and HIGH cook times, I have found that almost every dish cooks best on one or the other setting. The recipes in this book provide specific directions for the temperature that gives the best results. Generally, 1 hour of cooking on the HIGH setting equals 2 to 2½ hours on LOW.

Conventional Recipe Time	Slow Cooker Time on LOW
15 minutes	1½ to 2 hours
20 minutes	2 to 3 hours
30 minutes	3 to 4 hours
45 minutes	5 to 6 hours
60 minutes	6 to 8 hours
90 minutes	8 to 9 hours
2 hours	9 to 10 hours
3 hours	12 hours plus

damp, soapy sponge and dry with a towel. Make sure the bottom inside is clean and free of food particles or spillage.

Secrets of Slow Cooking: The Panic-Proof Pantry

You do not need to have a connoisseur's mentality to cook good food. But if you are a busy person, a good survival strategy is to have a well-stocked pantry to make meal preparation easy and avoid constantly having to run to the store to pick up ingredients.

The concept revolves around an update of the larder, whether cooking solo or for entertaining 10. But even in the most modest pantry these days it is not unusual to see canned coconut milk next to jarred salsa and spicy hot harissa next to *herbes de Provence,* extra-virgin olive oil alongside sesame oil and grape leaves. Oh, and then there are the many barbecue sauces, dried fruit varieties, and low-sodium condiments. If you cannot make your own stocks or do not have the inclination to do so, keep plenty of your favorite canned vegetable and chicken broth on hand. And also think about purchasing little bottles of red and white wine, and those tiny bottles of liquors, like rum.

Many slow cooker cooks comment on how important it is to stock your freezer with pre-portioned meats for the ultimate convenience. Seasonality affects meat, poultry, and fish, just like produce, as the supermarkets gear up for holiday supplies. At peak availability, prices are lower for such items as turkey parts in early winter, lamb in the spring, and duck and game birds in the fall and winter. Cuts of beef for entertaining are often on sale when shoppers are planning summer barbecues and holiday feasts. With the larger cuts, like brisket, chuck roast, and flank steak, ask the butcher to cut them into smaller portions suitable for two. Cook one portion and freeze the other to use within the next few months.

I have included in this recipe collection both very easy, quick-to-assemble recipes (boneless chicken breasts in two hours) and those that take a bit more time (cassoulet or lamb shanks). What all the recipes have in common, however, is that they rely on your pantry. My panic-proof slow cooker pantry is designed for on-the-spot slow cooking preparation and contains foods that are versatile and make vivid, delicious flavor combinations.

The Freezer

Meat: Individually wrapped boneless chicken breasts (the quintessential desperation cooking food), turkey wings for broth, osso buco, lamb shanks, veal or lamb stew meat, beef or pork ribs, pork tenderloins, chuck roasts cut to size, meatballs, and sausages can be thawed in the refrigerator or microwave.

Vegetables: Frozen artichoke hearts, pearl onions, petit peas, bell pepper strips, and spinach are all things you'll be grateful not to have to prep.

•• Guide to Internal Meat Temperatures ••

The most reliable way to tell when meat and poultry have reached a particular stage of done-ness is with an instant-read thermometer or accurate meat thermometer. I recommend these tools as basic equipment for testing meat doneness in every slow cooker kitchen. Use this chart as a guide.

Type of Meat	Rare	Medium	Well-Done
Beef	125° to 130°F	140° to 145°F	160°F
Veal	Not recommended	140° to 145°F	160°F
Lamb	130° to 140°F	140° to 145°F	160°F
Pork and Ham	Not recommended	145° to 150°F	160°F
Poultry and Game Birds	Not recommended	170° to 175°F	180°F

The Refrigerator

Standards: Butter, sour cream, and crème fraîche or yogurt are used for sauces. Keep bacon or pancetta on hand too for soups and stews, as well as vacuum-packed sausages.

Sauces and condiments: Low-sodium soy sauce, hot sauce, hoisin sauce, Asian plum sauce, Dijon mustard, Worcestershire sauce, and maple syrup all come in handy.

Vegetables: Keep durable cabbage, apples, potatoes, carrots, celery, garlic, shallots, onions, and turnips on hand for soups, vegetable dishes, and stews. Also stock lemons, limes, fresh Italian parsley, and fresh cilantro. (You can also freeze fresh herbs.)

Cheeses: Keep Parmigiano-Reggiano, aged Asiago, or Pecorino Romano on hand for grating. Goat cheese and cheddar are also good and versatile.

The Cupboard

Tomatoes: I use a lot of tomato products in my slow cooker recipes since they are a wonderful and versatile flavor medium. Canned commercial tomatoes come in a wide variety of preparations (whole, diced, pureed), and some ver-sions come in aseptic packaging. They are so convenient, and often they taste way better than fresh. Canned whole or diced peeled tomatoes are certainly better than out-of-season market ones. Keep dehydrated and olive oil–packed sun-dried tomatoes too. Tomato paste is useful for keeping sauces from being too thin, and always keep one good commercial tomato sauce on hand for those on-the-spot rib dishes or a ragù.

Beans: Stock up on canned cannellini (Italian white beans), red kidney beans, pinto beans, garbanzo beans, and black beans. Keep dried beans as well, including *flageolets verte,* black turtle beans, cranberry beans, navy beans, pintos, lentils, split peas, moong dal, and Great Northern beans.

Stock and broth: Chicken, beef, and vegetable broth are essential. Sample different canned and aseptically packaged varieties to find a favorite. If you indulge in homemade stock, store your stocks in appropriately sized containers in the freezer.

Dried mushrooms: Once only a gourmet item, dried mushrooms are now excellent everyday slow cooker ingredients. A well-stocked supermarket will carry an entire selection, usually in a corner of the produce department. Dried porcini and shiitake mushrooms might be found in the Asian food section. Dried mushrooms keep indefinitely and reconstitute easily for sauces, risottos, and stews. I never use canned mushrooms.

Dried pastas: While I use limited amounts of pasta in slow cooker dishes, since it tends to get gummy (orzo and macaroni or mini-penne are sometimes used) if not carefully prepared, pasta is one of the best side dishes for most sauces and stews. Fit the shape to your dish: linguine, spaghetti, or thin spaghetti for seafood pastas, and stubby macaroni like penne, fusilli,

gemelli, or shells for chunkier sauces, as well as egg noodles and Japanese udon noodles.

Rice: Rice is another delicious and staple side dish for slow cooker meals. Some recipes also feature rice, especially converted rice and wild rice, which hold up beautifully in the long cooking process. Italian Arborio and Vialone nano are used for slow cooker risottos and rice pudding. Keep white basmati, Japanese-style short-grain white rice (Calrose), short-grain brown rice, and wild rice on hand as the basics for a delicious starchy side dish.

Dried fruits: Apricots, prunes, raisins, dried apples, figs, dried cranberries, and dried tart cherries are great for Moroccan tagines and for accompanying pork roasts and many quick chicken dishes in the slow cooker.

Vinegars: Keep a variety on hand for splashing: red and white wine vinegars, white and dark balsamic vinegars, champagne vinegar, and apple cider vinegar.

Oils: I mostly use light and extra-virgin olive oil in my recipes. Walnut oil is a great all-purpose cooking oil and is nutritionally healthy, like olive oil.

Chocolate: Unsweetened chocolate and good old-fashioned Hershey bars are used for mole sauces.

Preserves, jams, jellies: Not just breakfast-toast fare! Orange marmalade is great for ribs and glazes.

Stock some uncommon flavors, like whole sour cherry preserves, currant jelly, quince jelly, and lime or ginger marmalade, all of which can end up as ingredients.

Cereals: Steel-cut oats, rolled oats, grits, polenta, and fresh stone-ground cornmeal (refrigerate this, please) can all be cooked in the slow cooker.

Essential sundries: Canned evaporated milk, your favorite barbecue sauce, jarred roasted red peppers, canned roasted green chiles, chipotles in adobo sauce, jarred salsa, tuna packed in olive oil or spring water, olives (green, black kalamata, canned ripe California), and capers all make good additions to sauces, soups, and stews. Many recipes also call for all-purpose flour, granulated sugar, and brown sugar.

• • High-Altitude Slow Cooking • •

While it is virtually impossible to overcook food in the slow cooker when cooked on LOW, there are guidelines for slow cooking at altitudes more than 3,000 feet above sea level. Just remember that the higher you go, the more compressed the air is, and liquids take longer to come to a boil. If you are at a high altitude, figure that your food will take approximately 25 percent more time to come up to the proper cooking temperature and to cook.

Just as oven temperatures need to be increased (the rule is to increase oven temperature by 1°F for every 100 feet of altitude) to compensate for slower heating at high altitudes, the slow cooker will run at a lower overall temperature at higher altitudes, so cook all foods on HIGH and increase the cooking time slightly. Use the LOW heat setting rather than the KEEP WARM setting for keeping food warm.

Use the following chart as a guideline. Be sure to note the adjustments you make to recipes for future cooking.

Adjustment	Altitude		
Cook all recipes on HIGH	3,000 feet	5,000 feet	7,000 to 8,000 feet
For each cup of liquid specified in the recipe, decrease by:	1 to 2 tablespoons	2 to 3 tablespoons	3 to 4 tablespoons

Hale and Hearty
Main-Dish Soups

Soup, beautiful soup. It is a specialty of my home kitchen. I always have some soup in the fridge, and I love to have a big bowl of comforting soup for a main dish. I usually make soup in the 3-quart cooker so that there is enough for two filling bowls and some leftovers for the next day or for freezing.

This collection of soups includes small-batch stocks, so delicious on their own, with a bit of pasta and vegetables tossed in, or as a base for your other soups in place of canned broth. Once you find out how simple it is to whip up a chicken broth or vegetable broth, you will never be without. They freeze beautifully, and they are especially tasty.

There is also a wide selection of thin purees and chowder-like vegetable soups in this chapter, some smooth, others chunky and thick like a potage. There are a number of soups made with potatoes, the mainstay of the home soup kitchen. There are soups with chicken and turkey, and bean and legume soups that include split peas and lentils. You will notice that I love black bean soups, a staple on the Yucatán peninsula and in Guatemala, Cuba, and Puerto Rico. I have included some of my all-time favorites, like bean with bacon. Please remember that with all bean, split pea, and lentil soups, add the salt at the end of cooking, not before, or else the beans will not cook properly.

I like to prepare soups that reflect a wide variety of global flavors, and come from distinct culinary cultures like Mexico and France, Scandinavia and China. I have some regional soups like minestrone from Italy and turkey and rice congee from China. In these recipes I went for comfort, value, simplicity of ingredients, and suitability for everyday cooking. I recommend that your kitchen arsenal include a nice soup ladle; it makes serving all the more pleasant.

Chicken Broth

H omemade chicken broth is a delight, and once you try it, you may view it as an essential ingredient in soups, risottos, and stews. This is so easy to make with just chicken wings, but you can break up the bones from your own roast chicken as well. My mother uses the leftover carcass from her favorite store-bought rotisserie chicken. Just drop everything into the crock and let it cook all day. The best stocks are never boiled, just simmered slowly so that they never get bitter, and the slow cooker is excellent at the job. Now there is no reason not to have your own stash of broth in the freezer. ○ *Makes 4 to 5 cups*

COOKER: 3 quart
SETTINGS AND COOK TIMES: HIGH for 1 hour, then LOW for 8 to 12 hours

1½ pounds chicken wings, chopped in half at the joints
1 medium-size yellow onion, peeled and quartered
2 stalks celery with leaves, cut into chunks
4 sprigs fresh Italian parsley
A few grinds of fresh black pepper or a few whole black peppercorns
½ bay leaf
Salt to taste

1. Place all of the ingredients, except for the salt, into the slow cooker. Add water to cover by 2 to 3 inches. Cover and cook on HIGH for 1 hour.

2. Uncover and skim off the foam on the surface. Cover, reduce heat setting to LOW, and cook for 8 to 12 hours. If the water cooks down below the level of the ingredients, add a bit of boiling water.

3. Uncover and let cool to lukewarm. Set a large colander lined with cheesecloth or a fine mesh strainer over a large bowl and pour the broth through to strain. Press down on the vegetables to extract all the liquid. Discard the vegetables, skin, and bones. Taste the stock and add salt to taste.

4. The broth is ready for use and can be refrigerated, tightly covered, for up to 3 days. The fat will separate and rise to the top; scoop off with a spoon and discard. Or divide the stock into airtight storage containers, leaving 2 inches at the top to allow for expansion, and freeze for up to 3 to 4 months.

Basic Vegetable Broth

Vegetable stock is increasingly common now alongside chicken and beef stocks. It is a homemade delight that freezes well, and it is really easy to make in the slow cooker. Some people make it twice a week and have it on hand all the time. It has a decidedly neutral taste and can be used in place of meat or poultry broth in any recipe. It can reflect the seasons by varying the ingredients. Use leek tops, tomato ends, spinach and parsley stems, and green bean strings. I use fresh vegetables for each batch of vegetable stock, unless the vegetable trimmings are not more than a day old; older vegetables just do not cook up into a nice-tasting stock. Note that cruciferous vegetables that have strong flavors should not be used. This includes broccoli, kale, the cabbage family, turnips, Brussels sprouts, and cauliflower: They will flavor your stock distinctly, even make it bitter and sulfurous. Potatoes make a stock murky from their starch, and beets will instantly tint your stock, so it is best to leave these out as well. ○ *Makes 4 to 5 cups*

COOKER: 3 quart
SETTINGS AND COOK TIMES: HIGH for 1 hour, then LOW for 5 to 6 hours

1 medium-size yellow onion, peeled and quartered
1 leek, well rinsed and chopped
½ carrot or parsnip, cut into chunks
3 stalks celery with leaves, cut into chunks
4 or 5 whole green beans
1 small tomato, halved
2 ounces fresh mushrooms, or 1 to 2 dried mushrooms
1 clove garlic, cut in half
4 sprigs fresh Italian parsley
2 sprigs fresh cilantro
½ bay leaf
1 long strip lemon peel
4 whole black peppercorns
2 allspice berries
Assorted seasonal vegetables as desired, such as corncobs, wild mushrooms,
    fennel, or basil stems
Salt to taste

1. Place all of the ingredients, except for the salt, into the slow cooker. Add water to cover by 2 to 3 inches. Cover and cook on HIGH for 1 hour.

2. Reduce the heat setting to LOW and simmer for 5 to 6 hours. If the water cooks down below the level of the ingredients, add a bit of boiling water.

3. Uncover and let cool to lukewarm. Set a large colander or strainer with a double layer of cheesecloth over a large bowl and pour the broth through to strain. Press down on the vegetables to extract all the liquid. Discard the vegetables. Add salt to taste.

4. The broth is ready for use and can be refrigerated, tightly covered, for up to 3 days. Or divide the stock into airtight storage containers, leaving 2 inches at the top to allow for expansion, and freeze for up to 3 months.

·· Slow Cooker Tip: What Not to Cook ··

Certain foods are emphatically not suitable for slow cooking. These include tender steaks, large loin roasts such as prime rib, poultry with the skin on (this triples the fat content of the dish), pies and cookies, layer cakes, pasta (except for orzo and some recipes with small tube pastas, such as soups), most rice (except for converted rice, which holds its shape during long cooking, wild rice, and risotto), fresh delicate seafood, and cheese and dairy products like milk and sour cream (use evaporated milk, or else add regular dairy products during the last hour of cooking). I never place frozen foods directly in the slow cooker unless a recipe specifically calls for it, as it throws off the heating of the contents. Never thaw foods of any type in the slow cooker.

Delicious Turkey Broth

urkey stock is one of my favorite broths, but it is often quite a hassle since you must have some nice bones to make it. Well, this stock recipe, using wings and legs, will give you the ability to make turkey stock year round with the ease of making chicken broth. You can use all wings if you like; they have plenty of meat to flavor the broth. If you like a really rich broth, brown the pieces first. For this, you roast the turkey parts and vegetables in a 400°F oven until nicely browned, or sauté them with some olive oil in a skillet, then proceed with the recipe. ○ *Makes about 5 cups*

COOKER: 3 quart
SETTINGS AND COOK TIMES: HIGH for 1 hour (optional), then LOW for 8 to 12 hours

About 1½ pounds turkey parts (preferably wings,
    but legs and other bony parts are good)
1 medium-size yellow onion, unpeeled, cut in half, and each half stuck
    with 1 whole clove
1 carrot or parsnip, cut into chunks
2 stalks celery with leaves, cut in half crosswise
6 sprigs fresh Italian parsley
¼ teaspoon dried thyme or 1 sprig fresh thyme
1 to 2 cloves garlic, smashed flat with side of a knife
¼ teaspoon whole black peppercorns
1 bay leaf
Salt to taste

1. Place all of the ingredients, except for the salt, into the slow cooker and add water to cover by 2 inches. Cover and cook on HIGH for 1 hour, if you like, or start on LOW.

2. Uncover and skim off the foam on the surface with a large spoon. Cover, reduce heat setting to LOW, and simmer for 8 to 12 hours. If the water cooks down below the level of the ingredients, add a bit of boiling water.

3. Uncover and let cool to lukewarm. Set a large colander or strainer with a double layer of cheesecloth over a large bowl and pour the broth through to strain.

Press down on the vegetables to extract all the liquid. Discard the vegetables and bones. Remove and chop the meat; store the meat separately in a plastic bag for another use. Add salt to taste.

4. The broth is ready for use and can be refrigerated, tightly covered, for up to 3 days. Remove congealed fat, if any, from the surface. Or divide the stock into airtight storage containers, leaving 2 inches at the top to allow for expansion, and freeze for up to 3 months.

• • About Your Slow Cooker Broths • •

A stock or broth is a clear, unseasoned soup made by simmering bones and vegetables to extract their essential flavors. Homemade broths are vastly superior to anything you can buy commercially. Slow cookers are known for making fantastic broths—you put in the ingredients, cover with water, and let the cooker do all the work. Usually broths are made in large quantities, but with the 3- to 3½-quart cooker, a small amount can be made for just one soup, or for freezing in convenient quantities. I know cooks who use only their own homemade broths and keep a stash of them in the freezer at all times. Once you find out how easy they are to prepare in the slow cooker, you will make them yourself as well.

Please note that the recipes never call for salt during preparation. If you added salt during the cooking, it would get too concentrated and you would end up with an overly salty broth. Add salt only at the end of preparation.

After they have cooled, your broths can be covered and refrigerated for a few days. This is when you can lift off and discard any congealed fat from the surface. If your broth needs to be refreshed after a few days, place it in a saucepan, bring to a boil, and let cool before refrigerating again. This will extend the life of your broth.

For long-term storage, partially fill heavyweight, zipper-top freezer bags in portions—use both 1-pint and 1-quart bags. Do not fill the bags more than three-quarters full, to allow for expansion while freezing. I lay the bags flat for easy stacking. I also label the bags with the type of broth and the date. To defrost, simply remove the block of frozen stock from the bag to a saucepan or microwave-safe bowl and slowly heat until melted. Then add to your soup or stew; do not add frozen broth to the slow cooker, since it will slow the cooking time dramatically. If you have defrosted too much broth, just reheat it to boiling, then cool and refreeze.

Zucchini Soup with Oven Croutons

I adore zucchini soup with a hint of curry, and this one comes from a magazine article from the 1960s featuring an interview with the late Katharine Hepburn, in which she gave a recipe for her favorite soup. Here it is, but made in the slow cooker. You can serve this hot with the chives and croutons, or chill it a few hours to overnight and serve it cold, which is wonderful on a hot day. The croutons, though, are best served on the day they are made. I have been known to splurge with a dollop of sour cream too, but the soup is perfect without it. ● *Serves 2*

COOKER: 3 quart
SETTING AND COOK TIME: LOW for 5 to 6 hours

¼ cup (½ stick) unsalted butter

3 shallots, finely chopped

2 pounds zucchini, ends trimmed and thickly sliced

4 cups chicken broth, canned or homemade (see page 17)

1½ teaspoons curry powder

1⅛ teaspoons salt

⅛ teaspoon cayenne pepper

OVEN CROUTONS:

2 slices fresh or day-old bread

2 to 3 tablespoons melted unsalted butter or olive oil, or a combination

2 tablespoons minced fresh chives

1. In a large skillet over medium-high heat, melt the butter, then cook the shallots and zucchini for about 3 minutes, just to soften and coat the vegetables with the butter. Place in the slow cooker and add the broth, curry powder, salt, and cayenne pepper. Cover and cook on LOW for 5 to 6 hours.

2. While the soup is cooking, make the croutons. Preheat the oven to 375°F. If the bread is soft, cut into thick cubes; if dense, cut into smaller cubes. Place on an ungreased baking sheet and drizzle the cubes with the melted butter or olive oil; toss with your hands to coat evenly. Bake for 10 to 15 minutes, until crisp and golden. Remove from the oven and set aside to cool.

3. Using a handheld immersion blender, or transferring to a food processor or blender in batches, puree the soup. Ladle the hot soup into bowls and sprinkle with the chives and croutons.

Mushroom Barley Soup with Nasturtium Butter

On one of my birthdays, I went to dinner at the highly celebrated Greens Restaurant in San Francisco. When I ordered the mushroom barley soup with a dab of nasturtium butter as my first course, I thought I was getting an Old World favorite, but instead I was treated to an incredible updated taste treat. The mushroom soup was dark and rich, despite having no meat broth. I had to crack the code, and I was rewarded with the fact that the soup boasted dried porcini mushrooms along with fresh mushrooms. Since that epiphany, I have enjoyed my own version of that splendid mushroom soup many times with a side of onion focaccia, just like in the restaurant. Here it is, re-created for you in the slow cooker. Look for dried mushrooms in the produce department of a well-stocked supermarket or in bulk at the deli counter. If you make the nasturtium butter, plan to make it at the same time you are loading the slow cooker so that the flavors have time to meld. The butter will take on the summer perfume of the flowers and taste very rich. ◦ *Serves 2*

COOKER: 3 quart
SETTING AND COOK TIME: LOW for 6 to 7 hours

6 cups vegetable broth, canned or homemade (see page 18; can be roasted vegetable broth)
3 shallots, finely chopped
1 pound fresh white mushrooms, stems trimmed and thickly sliced
½ ounce dried porcini mushrooms, broken up
1 medium-size carrot, diced
2 stalks celery, diced
½ cup pearl barley
½ teaspoon dried thyme
Salt and freshly ground black pepper to taste

NASTURTIUM BUTTER:
¼ cup (½ stick) unsalted butter, at room temperature
1 to 2 small freshly picked unsprayed whole nasturtium flowers, rinsed, patted dry, and chopped

1. Place all of the ingredients except for the salt and pepper into the slow cooker. Cover and cook on LOW for 6 to 7 hours. Season to taste with salt and pepper.

2. To make the nasturtium butter, cream the butter with a fork in a small bowl or in a mini food processor until fluffy. Gently mash in the nasturtiums until evenly combined. Cover and refrigerate for up to 24 hours.

3. Ladle the hot soup into bowls, top with a little dab of the flavored butter, and serve immediately. Freeze or refrigerate any leftover nasturtium butter for another use.

Butternut Squash Soup

I adore pumpkin soup, but butternut squash soup is even better. In the realm of the hard winter squashes, butternut is unequaled in appealing sweet flavor. Here it is combined with apples and shallots. You can cook your own squash in the oven or use frozen squash with no loss of flavor. No cream is necessary, as the squash is creamy by nature. If you are serving this to company, whip $\frac{1}{2}$ pint heavy cream and add $\frac{1}{2}$ teaspoon curry powder; it is a surprising and delicious topper to this soup. Serve with nice dinner rolls, such as Parker House.

○ *Serves 2*

COOKER: 3 quart
SETTING AND COOK TIME: LOW for 4 to 5 hours

3 tablespoons unsalted butter
3 shallots, finely chopped
$\frac{2}{3}$ cup diced peeled apple
Three 12-ounce packages frozen cooked butternut squash, thawed and
    drained, or 4 to 4$\frac{1}{2}$ cups fresh butternut squash puree
2$\frac{1}{2}$ to 3 cups chicken broth, canned or homemade (see page 17)
$\frac{1}{2}$ teaspoon ground ginger
$\frac{1}{4}$ cup dry white wine
1 teaspoon salt
A few grinds of black pepper

1. In a large skillet over medium heat, melt the butter and cook the shallots and apple for about 3 minutes, just to soften and coat them with the butter. Place in the slow cooker and add the squash, broth, ginger, wine, and salt. Cover and cook on LOW for 4 to 5 hours.

2. Using a handheld immersion blender, or transferring to a food processor or blender in batches, puree the soup. Ladle the hot soup into bowls, sprinkle with the pepper, and serve hot.

Cauliflower Soup

Cauliflower soup was a favorite of Madame DuBarry, one of the famous courtesans in French history, and I am sure a delicate *chou-fleur* soup velouté graced many a cauldron at Versailles and Fontainebleau (the soup also carries her name now). Cauliflower, whose name comes from the Latin *caulis* (stalk) and *floris* (flower), is creamy white and the most sophisticated member of the cabbage family. The tight flower, referred to as the curd, is completely edible and makes a marvelous soup when broken up into little florets. Served with French bread, this is French peasant food at its most elemental. ❍ *Serves 2*

COOKER: 3 quart
SETTING AND COOK TIME: LOW for 6 to 7 hours

2 medium-size leeks (white parts only), ends trimmed and thinly sliced
1 medium-size russet potato, peeled and diced
1 small- to medium-size head cauliflower or Romanesco cauliflower, broken into florets
4 cups water, chicken broth, or vegetable broth, canned or homemade (see page 17 or 18),
  to cover
2 tablespoons olive oil
Salt to taste
Milk (optional) to thin the soup
Extra-virgin olive oil (optional) for drizzling

1. Place the leeks, potato, and cauliflower into the slow cooker. Add the water and olive oil to the crock. Cover and cook on LOW for 6 to 7 hours, until the potato and cauliflower are tender.

2. Using a handheld immersion blender, or transferring to a food processor or blender in batches, puree the soup. Add salt to taste and add some milk to thin the soup, if you like. Ladle the hot soup into bowls, drizzle with some extra-virgin olive oil, if you like, and serve immediately.

Provençal Tomato Soup
with Poached Eggs

From a French friend in Provence comes this lovely peasant soup with poached eggs floating in it, flavored ever so gently with saffron, fennel, and orange. You can offer one or two poached eggs per person, depending on appetites. All you need is a fresh green salad and some crusty bread to make this a great dinner. Don't skip the chopped parsley at the end—it adds a lot of flavor.

○ *Serves 2*

COOKER: 3 quart
SETTING AND COOK TIME: HIGH for 3 to 3½ hours

One 28-ounce can whole plum tomatoes, crushed and undrained
1 small yellow onion, coarsely chopped
1 or 2 cloves garlic, to your taste, minced
1 medium-size red or white new potato, cubed, or ½ cup cooked white or brown long-grain rice
3 tablespoons olive oil
3 strips orange zest, about 2 inches long by ½ inch wide
Pinch of saffron threads
¼ teaspoon chopped fresh thyme leaves
⅛ teaspoon fennel seed, crushed in a mortar and pestle
⅛ teaspoon sugar
¼ teaspoon salt
Pinch of cayenne pepper
2 to 4 eggs
3 to 4 tablespoons chopped fresh Italian parsley
Extra-virgin olive oil (optional) for drizzling

1. Place the tomatoes, onion, garlic, potato, olive oil, orange zest, saffron, thyme, fennel seed, sugar, salt, and cayenne pepper into the slow cooker. Cover and cook on HIGH for 3 to 3½ hours. The soup will be quite thick, but you can thin with a bit of hot water or chicken broth if you like.

2. Remove the strips of orange zest and discard. Break each egg into a heatproof cup. Lower the cup into the soup so the egg can flow out gently. You will easily be able to cook 2 eggs at once; if you have an oval cooker, 4 will fit; otherwise cook in 2 shifts. Cover and set a timer for 5 minutes for runny yolks, 7 minutes for firmer yolks. (You can test them for doneness by gently pressing each yolk with a spoon.)

3. To serve, use a slotted spoon to gently slip a poached egg into the bottom of each shallow soup bowl. Ladle the hot soup over the egg, sprinkle with parsley, drizzle with olive oil, if desired, and serve immediately.

Curried Cream of Broccoli Soup

B roccoli (from the Italian word *brocco,* for "shoot" or "stalk") works beautifully in this simple, hearty, and delightfully economical vegetable chowder. Broccoli is a member of the cruciferous family, along with cauliflower, cabbage, and mustard greens, all known for their characteristic aroma, indicating the concentration of a healthful phytonutrient called sulforaphane. While most people go for the hundreds of miniature flower buds in each section, called a floret, I love the flavor and texture of the stems better, so use them as well. Be sure to cook this soup on LOW after adding the broccoli to preserve the vegetable's flavor and bright green color. ❍ *Serves 2*

COOKER: 3 quart
SETTINGS AND COOK TIMES: HIGH for 2 hours, then LOW for 2 hours

½ to ¾ pound broccoli
4 cups low-sodium chicken broth or vegetable broth, canned or homemade (see page 17 or 18)
1 small yellow onion, diced
1 small leek (white part only), sliced
2 medium-size boiling potatoes, peeled and diced
1 medium-size carrot, coarsely grated
¾ to 1 teaspoon curry powder, to your taste
¼ teaspoon ground cumin
Pinch of cayenne pepper
About ½ cup regular or reduced-fat sour cream
½ teaspoon salt, or to taste
Juice and zest of 1 lime

1. Prepare the broccoli by cutting off the florets and chopping into 1-inch pieces; peel and chop the stems. Peel the main stem and thinly slice, discarding the bottom 2 inches. Set aside.

2. Place the broth, onion, leek, potatoes, and carrot into the slow cooker. Cover and cook on HIGH for 2 hours, until the potatoes are tender.

3. Add the broccoli, curry powder, cumin, and cayenne pepper. Reduce the heat to LOW, cover, and cook for about 2 hours, until the broccoli is barely tender and still bright green.

4. Using a handheld immersion blender, or transferring to a food processor or blender in batches, puree the soup. You want it sort of coarse, with bits of carrot and broccoli evident. Stir in the sour cream and add the salt and lime juice and zest. Serve immediately.

Power Outages

If you are not at home during the entire cooking process and the power goes out, throw away the food, even if it looks done. If you are at home, finish cooking the ingredients immediately by some other means: on a gas stove, on the outdoor grill, or at a house where the power is on. If the food was completely cooked just as the power went out, it should remain safe for up to two hours in the cooker with the power off.

Fennel Potato Leek Soup

This is a variation of the venerable potato leek soup that is as French as the Eiffel Tower; it is a combination of leeks and potatoes with a small proportion of fennel tossed in. The fennel has a faint licorice flavor that is nicely balanced by the potatoes. Leeks are much milder in taste than regular onions and make a superior-tasting broth. Be sure to clean the leeks well under running water, as there can be sand in the layers; split them lengthwise and rinse as you pull the layers open. This is home cooking at its best; it tastes just as good made with water as with broth. You just cook the vegetables until they are mushy, puree, and *voilà!* You can add the milk or not, depending on your mood. Grilled cheddar cheese sandwiches go great with this soup, as does plain French bread.

○ *Serves 2*

COOKER: 3 quart
SETTING AND COOK TIME: HIGH for 4 to 6 hours

1 large leek (white part only), end trimmed and thinly sliced
½ cup diced fresh fennel
2 large russet potatoes, peeled and diced
2 tablespoons chopped fresh Italian parsley
4 to 6 cups water, chicken broth, or vegetable broth, canned or homemade (see page 17 or 18)
Pinch of cayenne pepper
Salt to taste
1 tablespoon unsalted butter
1 cup plain soymilk or low-fat milk (optional)

1. Place the leek, fennel, potatoes, and parsley into the slow cooker. Add the water to the crock, just to cover (if you are also adding milk, use the lesser amount of water; if not, add the full 6 cups). Cover and cook on HIGH for 4 to 6 hours, until the potatoes are tender.

2. Using a handheld immersion blender, or transferring to a food processor or blender in batches, puree the soup. Sprinkle in the cayenne pepper, add salt to taste, and swirl in the butter. Stir in the milk, if you like. Serve immediately.

Sopa de Casera with Chicken, Tofu, Avocado, and Beans

This homemade soup uses some of my favorite tasty Mexican ingredients— bits of cooked chicken, cilantro, tomato, beans, rice, and lime. With its warm flavors and bright colors, it can give a chilly, dark day a festive summer feeling. Serve with warm plain or whole wheat tortillas with butter. o *Serves 2*

COOKER: 3 quart
SETTING AND COOK TIME: HIGH for about 3 hours

½ cup chopped white onion

1 clove garlic, minced

¼ cup plus 3 tablespoons chopped fresh cilantro leaves

2 tablespoons uncooked long-grain white or brown rice or converted rice

1 cup canned baby white beans, Great Northern beans, or pinto beans, rinsed and drained

Pinch of crumbled dried oregano or marjoram

Pinch of red pepper flakes

3 cups chicken broth, canned or homemade (see page 17)

1 cup shredded rotisserie chicken meat

½ cup cubed extra-firm tofu

Pinch of salt

A few grinds of black pepper

½ cup chopped, seeded tomato

½ cup cubed avocado

Juice of 1 lime

2 tablespoons sour cream or *crema mexicana* thinned with some milk, for garnish

2 to 4 lime wedges for serving

1. Combine the onion, garlic, 3 tablespoons of the cilantro, rice, beans, oregano, red pepper flakes, and broth in the slow cooker. Cover and cook on HIGH for 3 hours, until the onions and rice are cooked.

2. Add the shredded chicken, tofu, remaining ¼ cup cilantro, and salt and pepper. Cover and cook for another 30 minutes.

3. Right before serving, stir in the tomato, avocado, and lime juice. Serve immediately, ladled into bowls and drizzled with a tablespoon of sour cream. Pass lime wedges for squeezing.

Chicken, Coconut, and Galangal Soup

Thai cuisine reflects a culinary philosophy that balances four essences—*prik*, *preco*, *khem*, and *wan*, better known as hot, sour, salty, and sweet. This is my favorite soup in all of Asian cooking, along with miso soup. The first time I had it homemade, my eyes opened wide from the delicious flavor and I had two big bowlfuls. In Thai restaurants it is a standard offering, but at times I am perturbed by the chunks of things I do not recognize, since the entire chicken is chopped up—bones, skin, and all—and put into the soup. Well, here is my version, and it is terrifically delicious, American style. You will probably have to shop at an Asian market to get certain ingredients, such as *nam pla* (fish sauce), lime leaves, lemongrass, and galangal root (a member of the ginger family—you can substitute fresh ginger), all essential to the taste of the brew. Please don't eat the chunks of galangal, the lime leaves, or the lemongrass; they are just flavoring agents. ○ *Serves 2*

COOKER: 3 quart
SETTING AND COOK TIME: HIGH for 2 to 3 hours; chiles added after 1½ hours

4 cups low-sodium chicken broth, canned or homemade (see page 17)
⅓ cup freshly squeezed lime juice
4 kaffir lime leaves, broken in half
One 4-inch piece lemongrass, lower stalk only, bruised or flattened,
    then chopped into a few pieces
One 2-inch piece galangal, split lengthwise into several pieces
4 to 6 tablespoons Thai fish sauce *(nam pla)*, to your taste
6 to 8 ounces boneless, skinless chicken breast, thinly sliced
One 13.5-ounce can unsweetened coconut milk
2 small red chiles, slightly crushed but left whole
¼ cup fresh cilantro leaves for garnish

1. Heat the broth in the microwave and pour into the slow cooker. Add the lime juice, lime leaves, lemongrass, galangal, fish sauce, chicken, and coconut milk. Cover and cook on HIGH for 2 to 3 hours, until steaming hot and fragrant and the chicken is cooked through. Add the red chiles 1½ hours into the cooking time.

2. Remove and discard the lemongrass, lime leaves, and galangal. Ladle the hot soup into small, deep bowls, sprinkle with cilantro leaves, and serve immediately.

Turkey and Rice Congee (Jook)

The slow cooker makes fantastic, creamy *jook* (pronounced "juk"), the soothing and slightly salty savory rice porridge. It is a sustaining dish eaten as a dinner or lunch soup, as well as a before-bed snack or a simple but different breakfast. I love how easy this soup is—just toss everything into the crock and let it cook all day (or night). It's a staple in China and has become an increasingly popular menu item in the United States. Chinese Americans especially love a *jook* made with turkey stock. Instead of making a separate stock, I've just used a turkey wing here to flavor the broth. Serve with bowls of condiments on the side—chopped cilantro or parsley, minced green onion, soy sauce, and any hot chili sauce. ● *Serves 2*

COOKER: 3 quart
SETTINGS AND COOK TIMES: HIGH for 1 hour, then LOW for 6 to 8 hours

⅔ cup uncooked long-grain white rice
1 turkey wing (12 to 16 ounces)
6 cups water
1½ teaspoons salt
One 1½-inch piece peeled fresh ginger
Chopped fresh cilantro or Italian parsley leaves for garnish
Minced green onion for garnish
Low-sodium soy sauce for garnish
Hot red chili sauce of your choice for garnish

1. Place the rice, turkey wing, water, salt, and ginger into the slow cooker. Stir well. Cover and cook on HIGH for 1 hour, then reduce the temperature to LOW and cook for 6 to 8 hours, until creamy, thick, and translucent white in consistency.

2. Remove and discard the chunk of ginger. Remove the turkey wing and place on a plate to cool for 15 minutes. Remove and discard the skin. Pick the meat off the bones and discard the bones; return the meat to the soup. Keep on WARM until ready to serve, with bowls of the cilantro, green onion, soy sauce, and chili sauce on the side for garnish.

Turkey Minestrone

his is a delightful version of minestrone, originally from a recipe by Distel brand turkey and here adapted for the slow cooker. I had never made a nice vegetable soup with an Italian flair with turkey as its base, but it is a natural flavor pairing you will make often. I use different pasta each time—regular semolina pasta, whole wheat pasta, or even rice pasta, all available in dried form. Stay away from fresh pasta in soups, as it tends to disintegrate into the broth; dried pasta will keep its shape. You must make the turkey broth at least one day ahead, so plan accordingly. o *Serves 2*

COOKER: 3 quart

SETTING AND COOK TIME: LOW for about 8 hours (optional to cook on HIGH for 1 hour to start); turkey and beans added after 6 hours

1 medium-size yellow onion, chopped

2 small stalks celery with leaves, chopped

2 small carrots or parsnips, sliced

1 large red potato, diced

1 cup savoy cabbage, chopped

1 cup green beans, cut into 1-inch pieces

1 small zucchini, diced

One 14.5-ounce can Italian-style tomatoes, undrained and broken up

3 cups turkey broth, canned or homemade (see page 20)

1 cup chopped cooked turkey meat (reserved from making broth)

1 cup canned cannellini beans, rinsed and drained

1 teaspoon dried basil or marjoram

Salt and freshly ground black pepper to taste

½ cup pasta, such as penne or little shells, cooked according to package directions

1. Place all of the vegetables, including the tomatoes and their liquid, and the turkey broth in the slow cooker. Cover and cook on LOW for 6 hours (you can cook for 1 hour on HIGH to start, if you like).

2. Add the turkey meat, beans, and basil; cover and continue to cook for another 2 hours, until the potatoes are tender.

3. When done, add salt and pepper to taste, along with the hot drained pasta. Serve immediately.

White Bean Soup with Bacon

Since I was a child, my favorite soup has been canned bean with bacon. I loved it so much I think I might have eaten it every day while growing up. Here is that sentimental favorite made from scratch, and it is just as good as I remember, maybe better. Note that the bacon must be cooked before adding it to the soup. ○ *Serves 2*

COOKER: 3 quart
SETTING AND COOK TIME: LOW for 8 to 9 hours

1 heaping cup dried Great Northern beans or baby white beans,
    soaked overnight and drained
1 medium-size yellow onion, finely chopped
1 carrot, diced
2 cloves garlic, chopped
½ cup tomato sauce
5 cups chicken broth, canned or homemade (see page 17)
3 ounces smoked bacon, diced
Salt and freshly ground black pepper to taste

1. Place the beans, onion, carrot, garlic, tomato sauce, and broth in the slow cooker. In a small frying pan, cook the bacon until golden and a bit crisp; drain and transfer to the crock. Cover and cook on LOW for 8 to 9 hours, until the beans are tender.

2. Season to taste with salt and pepper, and adjust the consistency if desired with hot water or more hot broth. Serve hot.

Winter Split Pea Soup

This is the soup you start making right after breakfast to have it ready for dinner. Be sure to get a nice, meaty smoked pork chop. It is already fully cooked and it adds a wonderful full flavor to your soup. Serve hot with warm bread or croutons. ○ *Serves 2*

COOKER: 3 quart
SETTING AND COOK TIME: LOW for 8 to 10 hours;
    petit peas added during last 30 minutes

1²/₃ **cups green split peas, rinsed and picked over**
5 **cups chicken broth, canned or homemade (see page 17)**
1 **small yellow onion, finely chopped**
1 **medium-size carrot, diced**
1 **stalk celery, diced**
1 **bay leaf**
1 **smoked pork chop (or leftover bone from a small ham)**
½ **cup frozen petit green peas, thawed**
Salt to taste

1. Place the split peas in the slow cooker; add the broth, onion, carrot, celery, and bay leaf. Stir to combine. Nestle the pork chop into the center of the crock. Cover and cook on LOW for 7½ to 9½ hours, until the split peas are completely tender.

2. Remove and discard the bay leaf. Remove the pork chop and shred the meat off the bone; discard the bone and set aside the meat. Using an immersion blender, or transferring to a food processor or blender, puree the soup, if you like a smooth soup; you can leave it chunky if you prefer. Return meat to the soup; add the petit peas and cook for another 30 minutes. Season to taste with salt, and serve hot.

Yellow Split Pea Soup with Cumin and Lemon

This is one of my favorite soups. I have been making it for more than 20 years and originally got the recipe from *The Tassajara Recipe Book* by Ed Brown (Shambhala, 1985). I serve it with steamed basmati rice, lemon wedges, and warm, buttered handmade tortillas. ● *Serves 2*

COOKER: 3 quart
SETTING AND COOK TIME: LOW for 8 to 10 hours

2 tablespoons unsalted butter
1 tablespoon olive oil
1 medium-size yellow onion, chopped
1 medium-size carrot, peeled, halved lengthwise, and diced
2 large stalks celery, chopped
1½ teaspoons ground cumin
1½ cups yellow split peas, rinsed and picked over
5 cups water
Two 1-inch-thick slices ginger, peeled and minced
1 bay leaf
Grated zest and juice of 1 large or 2 small lemons
1½ teaspoons salt, or more to taste
¼ teaspoon freshly ground black pepper
1 recipe Spicy Lemon Yogurt (optional) for serving (recipe follows)

1. In a large skillet, heat the butter and oil over medium-high heat. Add the onion, carrot, and celery and cook until tender, about 5 minutes. Add the cumin; cook another few minutes so that the spice will release its flavor.

2. Place the split peas, water, ginger, and bay leaf in the slow cooker. Add the cooked vegetables and scrape the cumin-soaked oil into the crock with a spatula; stir to combine. Cover and cook on LOW for 8 to 10 hours, until the split peas are completely tender.

3. Remove and discard the bay leaf. Add the lemon zest and juice, salt, and pepper. Cover and cook 10 minutes longer. Serve in bowls topped with the lemon yogurt, if desired.

Spicy Lemon Yogurt

While I sometimes skip this for weeknight meals if I am pressed for time, it is easy to prepare, and it is a welcome flavor addition when stirred into the soup. ○ *Makes 1 cup*

1 cup thick plain yogurt
¼ teaspoon ground coriander
⅛ teaspoon paprika
½ teaspoon grated lemon zest
Few drops hot pepper sauce, such as Tabasco, or pinch of cayenne pepper
Pinch of salt

Place the yogurt in a small bowl and add the coriander, paprika, lemon zest, hot sauce, and salt. Stir with a whisk until smooth. Cover and refrigerate until ready to serve.

Tomato Lentil Soup

(B)ack in my college days, a friend told me about going to a French-club meeting where the teacher served a big pot of lentil soup. It was fantastic, she said. We marveled that neither one of us had ever heard about it before. As a new cook who was game to try everything, I set myself to making a pot of lentil soup. I got a bag of brown lentils at the supermarket and followed the recipe that was printed on the bag. I looked into the pot, and those lentils were sitting on the bottom of the pot like little stones, and were in such a small proportion to the amount of water. This couldn't be right, I thought. So I went back to the store and got another bag of lentils and poured the whole bag into the pot with the first bag. That soup took all day to cook. When I finally looked into the pot after a few hours, I was horrified to see this unbelievably thick mass. I couldn't even stir it, and it was expanding at a rapid rate, filling my soup pot and threatening the beyond. Instead of scooping it into the garbage (these were the days before garbage disposals in a rental unit), I began ladling the lentils into the toilet, flushing in between scoopfuls. The sad moral of this story is that one should never put cooked lentils down the toilet; the pipes just cannot take the stress. Needless to say, it was years before I discovered the following recipe and made a decent pot of lentil soup. ● *Serves 2*

COOKER: 3 quart
SETTING AND COOK TIME: LOW for 7 to 9 hours

• • Slow Cooker Tip: LOW Maintenance • •

If you are leaving the slow cooker unattended all day or night, it is best to cook on the LOW setting. That way, there is no chance your food will overcook. Most pot roasts, stews, soups, and chili cook best on LOW.

---

1 tablespoon extra-virgin olive oil

2 ounces pancetta, chopped

¾ cup brown lentils, rinsed and picked over

1 small onion, finely chopped

1 carrot, diced

1 stalk celery, diced

4 cups water

2 tablespoons tomato paste

½ bay leaf

½ teaspoon crumbled dried thyme or marjoram

1 teaspoon salt, or to taste

¼ teaspoon freshly ground black pepper, or to taste

1 to 2 tablespoons red wine vinegar

1. In a medium-size skillet, heat the oil over medium heat. Add the pancetta and cook until translucent, 5 minutes.

2. Place the lentils, onion, carrot, celery, water, tomato paste, bay leaf, and thyme into the slow cooker. Use a heat-resistant rubber spatula to scrape the pancetta into the crock; stir to combine. Cover and cook on LOW for 7 to 9 hours, until the lentils are completely soft.

3. Season the soup with the salt and pepper, then add the vinegar, starting with 1 tablespoon and adding more if desired. Serve hot.

Black Bean Soup with Sausage and Greens

Forgive me for loving this soup. It was a stovetop recipe originally from Manny Nial, a baker to the stars in Los Angeles who became famous for developing doughnuts with no sugar added. This soup uses canned black refried beans, which are delicious. Manny writes, "I am always looking for new ways to use the fantastic array of precooked sausages proliferating in the market these days. Black bean soup is one of my favorites, but I never find the time to prepare the beans. I use an andouille chicken and turkey sausage—feel free to use whatever you like. You can always increase the heat level by adding a spicy hot salsa as a garnish." This soup is really thick, with lots of greens and sausage in every bite. Enjoy it with some homemade bread. ○ *Serves 2*

COOKER: 1½ to 3 quarts
SETTING AND COOK TIME: HIGH for 2½ to 3 hours

2 teaspoons olive oil
2 precooked sausages, spicy or mild, cut into bite-size chunks
8 ounces greens, such as Swiss chard, stems removed and coarsely chopped
2½ cups chicken broth, canned or homemade (see page 17)
One 15-ounce can refried black beans
Salt to taste
Sour cream, tomato salsa, and lime wedges for serving

1. Heat the oil in a large skillet and brown the sausages a little. Add the greens and heat just to wilt.

2. Place the broth and refried beans in the slow cooker and stir to combine. Add the sausage and greens; stir to combine. Cover and cook on HIGH for 2½ to 3 hours.

3. Add salt to taste. Add some boiling water to thin the soup, if desired. Ladle into serving bowls and serve hot with the sour cream, salsa, and lime wedges in small bowls on the side.

Chipotle Black Bean Vegetable Soup

(M)ade with convenient canned black beans that can always be waiting in your pantry, this soup can be ready in time for lunch if you start it in the morning. Serve it topped with shredded cheddar cheese, a dollop of sour cream, and lime wedges. ○ *Serves 2*

COOKER: 1½ to 3 quarts
SETTING AND COOK TIME: HIGH for 3 to 3½ hours

Two 15-ounce cans black beans, rinsed and drained
1 large shallot or small onion, finely chopped
1 small carrot or parsnip, diced
1 stalk celery, diced
¼ cup minced red bell pepper
½ to 1 chipotle chile in adobo sauce, minced, or
    1 tablespoon chipotle paste (see page 119)
4 cups water or vegetable broth, canned or homemade (see page 18)
¼ teaspoon crumbled dried marjoram
⅛ teaspoon chili powder
⅛ teaspoon ground cumin
1 teaspoon salt, or to taste
Shredded Monterey Jack cheese, sour cream, and lime wedges for serving

1. Place all of the ingredients except for the salt and the toppings into the slow cooker; stir to combine. Cover and cook on HIGH for 3 to 3½ hours.

2. Add salt to taste. Add some boiling water to thin the soup, if desired. Ladle into serving bowls and serve hot with the cheese, sour cream, and lime wedges in small bowls on the side.

I love herbs, both dried and fresh, and the special aromatic flavor they impart to a dish. The basic rule in using dried herbs in the slow cooker is to use a bit less than usual and add them to the pot with the initial ingredients. Fresh herbs are more volatile and delicate over the long cooking process, tending to break down and dissipate their flavor, so I add them at the end, or add a portion during the cooking and the remainder at the end. The ultimate test, of course, is your taste buds; please adjust the recipe to your palate, especially if you like more or less flavoring. When substituting one for the other, the approximate proportion is to use a third the amount of the dried herbs that you would of fresh. That is, if a recipe calls for 1 tablespoon of minced fresh basil, you would substitute 1 teaspoon dried.

Some people love having a small kitchen garden with a sunny patch devoted to their favorite herbs. Chives, mint, oregano, parsley, and sage grow nicely in pots indoors all winter. Or you may be just as happy to buy your herbs in the produce section at the supermarket. I also adore buying dried herbs by mail order from Penzeys Spices (800-741-7787, www.penzeys.com).

The following is a list of my most-used fresh herbs:

Basil, oregano, marjoram, savory, sage, thyme, rosemary, and bay leaf: These are the herbs that are most frequently called for in Mediterranean and American cooking. California bay leaves are double the strength of Turkish bay leaves, so be sure to check which type you have to avoid too strong a flavor.

Tarragon, chervil, chives, and dill: These are very prevalent herbs in European cooking, especially the tarragon and chervil. Tarragon is best harvested before it flowers, and chive flowers are delicious.

Parsley: Parsley is an all-purpose herb that is best used fresh and is one of my basic herbs. I also always use flat-leaf Italian parsley, since it is less chewy and has a more mellow flavor than the curly variety.

Cilantro, also called coriander or Chinese parsley: This is an herb that transcends all boundaries. It is as at home in Chinese and Thai cuisine as it is in Mexican. It looks like a delicate type of parsley and tastes peppery and refreshing. I never use dried, only fresh.

The Great American Chili Pot

I like a lot of variety in my chili—one day I'll have white style, with white beans and chicken, another day I'll make it smoky hot, with ground beef and black beans, and on yet another day, I'll cook it up with no meat at all and just hominy and fresh vegetables. Some days I like it spicy hot, and other days, I want it just to hint at the combination of spices.

Chili is one of the great reasons to own a slow cooker. While it is wonderful party food for a crowd, it is just as easy to make a small pot of chili for two. And all chilies can be made a day or two ahead; they just get better as they sit. They also freeze perfectly.

A traditional peasant stew dish displaying the creativity and originality of its first cooks along the border of the United States and northern Mexico, chili may look Mexican, but it is not. It is purely American. The humble chili of the nineteenth-century cattle drives and outdoor rancho kitchens now makes a showing on diverse restaurant menus, but it remains a fiery, sloppy-looking homemade dish, characterized by a flavor and color combination of red chile powder and herbs like oregano and cumin, and even accents of cinnamon and cloves. For a mild chili, there are pinches of this and that. For the chili-heads, there is plenty of everything, plus hot sauce, jalapeños, and cayenne. And then there is the powerhouse of condiments that end up as toppings, which I adore piling on.

Chili stews appear with or without beans, with meat or without, with tomatoes or not. Purists wouldn't even consider making or eating a chili with beans, but I don't limit myself. While all sorts of beans show up in chili today, the traditional bean for chili is the pinto, also called the *frijol* bean or Mexican red bean. There are also chilies made with black turtle beans (a popular bean for vegetarian chilies due to its sweet flavor), Great Northerns and garbanzos (favorites in white chilies), rattlesnake beans (relatives of the pinto), cannellini beans, cranberry beans, and the mottled brown-and-cream Jacob's cattle beans. You can substitute any one of these varieties for the pinto or red kidney bean. Mixing two or three varieties is also popular, especially in vegetarian versions.

I have kept the following chilies simple, using easy-to-obtain chili powders and chile peppers. The most popular hot dried chile today is the complexly flavored chipotle, or smoked dried jalapeño, which is readily available canned in adobo sauce. Fresh green chiles, often conveniently roasted and canned, and jalapeño chiles *en escabeche,* or pickled, are also good in your chili. When handling fresh chiles, which are in varying degrees irritating to the skin, wear surgical gloves, and by all means, never rub your eyes or pop some into your mouth unthinkingly.

While most chilies are served with warm fresh corn or flour tortillas, there are versions served with biscuits, sopaipillas (little fried bread triangles), and, of course, all manner of cornbreads, a natural pairing. A hunk of homemade whole wheat bread or crusty French baguette certainly works as well.

Slow Cooker Shapes

The modern slow cooker employs two basic shapes of thick, sturdy stoneware—round and oval—based on the designs of the classic earthenware cooking pots used in European cookery. The shapes encourage condensation, and the tight-fitting lids protect the contents from evaporation. Both shapes provide superb vessels for slow cooking. It is important to remember to use less liquid when cooking in the slow cooker than for conventional cooking methods, since there is no evaporation. The key is to keep in mind the principles of self-basting: The condensation under the lid adds an extra ½ to 1 cup liquid during the cooking process, hence it steams the food.

Overnight Chicken and Bean Chili

T he last thing before you go to bed, stir together this almost-white chili. Let it cook overnight in the slow cooker, and in the morning you will be ready to fill wide-mouth lunch thermoses. You can serve this mild chili, mixed with cooked macaroni, to children. As with most chilies, the longer you let it simmer, the better it gets. ○ *Serves 2 with leftovers*

COOKER: 3 quart
SETTING AND COOK TIME: LOW for 7 to 9 hours

4 boneless, skinless chicken thighs
Salt and freshly ground black pepper to taste
One 15.5-ounce can crushed tomatoes in puree
One 15-ounce can Great Northern or anasazi beans, rinsed and drained
One 15-ounce can black beans, rinsed and drained
One 4-ounce can tomato sauce
One 4-ounce can diced roasted green chiles, drained
1 small yellow onion, chopped
½ to 1 whole red, green, or yellow bell pepper, chopped
1 clove garlic, minced
1 small jalapeño chile, seeded and minced
2 tablespoons beer, red or white wine, or water
2 to 3 teaspoons chili powder, or to taste
Pinch of dried oregano or marjoram
Pinch of ground cumin
Shredded sharp cheddar cheese for serving
Sour cream for serving
Crumbled saltines for serving

1. Rinse the chicken and pat dry. Sprinkle with salt and pepper. Cut into 1- to 2-inch pieces. Place in the slow cooker and add the crushed tomatoes and puree, Great Northern beans, black beans, tomato sauce, canned green chiles, onion, bell pepper, garlic, jalapeño, beer, chili powder, oregano, and cumin. Stir to combine. Cover and cook on LOW for 7 to 9 hours, stirring occasionally.

2. Serve the chili in bowls, topped with cheese, sour cream, and crumbled saltines.

Old-Fashioned Beef and Mushroom Chili with Chipotle

his is a very mild "gringo" chili with ground beef and red kidney beans. I also like it with either anasazi beans or cranberry beans (also known as Italian borlotti or brown beans), if I can find them canned. Serve with warm Olive Oil Corn Muffins (page 228). ○ *Serves 2 with leftovers*

COOKER: 3 quart
SETTING AND COOK TIME: LOW for 7 to 9 hours

3 tablespoons olive oil
1 small yellow onion, chopped
1 stalk celery, chopped
6 ounces shiitake mushrooms, sliced
½ pound lean ground beef
1 tablespoon chili powder, or to taste
One 15.5-ounce can crushed tomatoes in puree
2 tablespoons beer, wine, or water
3 to 4 teaspoons chipotle chile paste (see page 119), to your taste
1 teaspoon Worcestershire sauce
1 teaspoon sugar or honey
One 15-ounce can red kidney beans, cranberry beans, or anasazi beans, rinsed and drained
Salt and freshly ground black pepper to taste
Shredded sharp cheddar cheese for serving
Sliced avocado for serving
Sour cream for serving

1. In a large skillet over medium-high heat, heat the olive oil and cook the onion, celery, and mushrooms until limp. Add the ground beef and cook until the meat is brown. Sprinkle with some of the chili powder about halfway through cooking. Place in the slow cooker and add the tomatoes and their puree, beer, the rest of the chili powder, the chipotle chile paste, Worcestershire sauce, and sugar. Stir to combine. Cover and cook on LOW for 4 hours, stirring occasionally.

2. After 4 hours, add the beans and salt and pepper. Cover and cook for another 3 to 5 hours. The longer you let it simmer, the better it gets.

3. Serve the chili in bowls, topped with cheese, avocado slices, and sour cream.

Turkey Chili with Baby White Beans

Baby white beans are among my favorite beans; they have a great taste and texture without being too filling, and they blend so nicely with ground turkey meat. This is a variation of a chili in *Not Your Mother's Slow Cooker Cookbook,* so it has stood the test of time to be a favorite. Be sure to get ground dark turkey meat, as ground white turkey meat will become very dry during cooking. You can substitute regular tomato sauce for the red chile sauce if you cannot find it, but it is another touch I love. Use an excellent cocoa powder, such as Scharffen Berger or Valrhona; it will add a lot, flavorwise. ○ *Serves 2*

COOKER: 3 quart
SETTING AND COOK TIME: LOW for 7 to 8 hours; beans added after 3½ hours

2 teaspoons olive oil
½ medium-size yellow onion, chopped
¾ pound ground dark turkey
1 tablespoon mild chili powder
½ teaspoon ancho chile powder
½ teaspoon crumbled dried marjoram
½ teaspoon ground cumin
¼ bay leaf
2 teaspoons unsweetened natural cocoa powder
½ teaspoon salt, or to taste
Pinch of ground cinnamon
1 cup beef broth
¼ cup canned red chile sauce, such as Las Palmas brand
1 cup whole canned tomatoes
One 15-ounce can small white beans, rinsed and drained
Chopped red onion for serving
Chopped fresh cilantro for serving
Shredded Monterey Jack cheese for serving
Sliced avocado for serving
Lime wedges for serving
Sour cream for serving

1. In a large skillet over medium heat, heat the olive oil and cook the onion until limp, 1 minute. Add the turkey and cook, stirring, until the meat is no longer pink, 8 to 10 minutes. Place in the slow cooker. Stir in the chili powder, ancho chile powder, marjoram, cumin, bay leaf, cocoa powder, salt, cinnamon, broth, red chile sauce, and tomatoes. Break up the tomatoes with a wooden spoon. Cover and cook on LOW for 3½ hours.

2. At 3½ hours, stir in the beans; cover and cook for another 3½ to 4½ hours.

3. Serve the chili in bowls with the red onion, cilantro, cheese, avocado, lime wedges, and sour cream in small bowls on the side.

• • Slow Cooker Tip: Handling Leftovers • •

The convenience of the slow cooker means that you can prepare extra-large batches of your favorite dishes, especially soups and stews. This allows for leftovers to refrigerate or freeze for another meal. Handle your leftover slow cooker foods with the same intelligence as you would oven and stovetop foods. Do not leave food in the stoneware crock at room temperature for long periods. Remove the contents, store the leftovers in shallow covered containers, and refrigerate within two hours after cooking is finished. Reheating leftovers in a slow cooker is not recommended. Use the stovetop or a microwave oven for the full reheat, and then, if you wish, place into a slow cooker to keep hot for serving.

Pushpa's Chili

Pushpa is my friend Raja Gursahani's mother, and she is known as a fabulous cook (she used to co-own a restaurant with her son), so I had to have Raj entice her to give me her slow cooker chili recipe. I used to make half this recipe, thinking it would be a better portion for two, but once I got addicted, a small bowl did not suffice anymore. I needed to be sure there were leftovers. If you have never bought canned chili beans before, be prepared for a surprise: They are tender to the point of being buttery and are an excellent addition to chili rather than using plain beans. This is a mild chili, suitable for children and people who normally may not care for chili. ● *Serves 2 with leftovers*

COOKER: 3 quart
SETTINGS AND COOK TIMES: HIGH for 1 hour, then LOW for 4 to 6 hours

2 pounds lean ground chuck or ground dark turkey
1 medium-large red onion, chopped
2 small ripe tomatoes, seeded and chopped
2 medium-size green bell peppers, stemmed, seeded, and chopped
Two 15.5-ounce cans chili beans in mild or spicy sauce, undrained
½ teaspoon ground cumin
½ teaspoon hot paprika (can be smoked paprika), ancho chile powder, or
    New Mexican chile powder
Salt to taste
Shredded sharp cheddar cheese for serving

1. In a large skillet over medium-high heat, cook the meat until the juices have evaporated and the meat has browned; drain off any fat and discard. Place in the slow cooker and add the onion, tomatoes, bell pepper, beans, cumin, and paprika. Stir to combine. Cover and cook on HIGH for 1 hour, then reduce the heat to LOW and cook for 4 to 6 hours. The longer you let it simmer, the better it gets. Check the chili at 3 hours and, if it seems too dry, add some boiling water. Add salt.

2. Ladle the chili into big bowls and top with the cheese. Serve immediately.

•• Red Chile Powder and Masa Harina ••

Chili would not be chili without good seasoning. While many good chili recipes call for the blend called chili powder, that is not the same as pulverized red chile powder, which is the ground powder of a single variety of dried chile.

The brilliant red of chile powder comes from green New Mexico chiles that are left on the vine until fall, ripening into a fruity berry red, then sun-dried and hung in ristras on porches. Real chile powder is simply crushed and powdered from these dried chiles. These are the same red chiles that are used to make red pepper flakes and Tabasco sauce. The chiles are grown all around New Mexico, and usually the package will indicate where the chile was grown: Hatch, Chimayo, San Juan Pueblo, Dixon, etc. I got turned on to the difference in chile powders by my friend and consultant on everything culinary Mexican and Southwestern, Jacquie Hiquera McMahan. She has a serious affinity for Dixon red chile powder, the Rolls-Royce of ground chiles, because of its incomparable flavor. Referred to as "the salt of the Southwest," Dixon chile powder is not just for chilies, but for sprinkling on potatoes and mixing into meatloaf, stews, rubs, and red chile sauce.

I also adore the flavor of ancho chile powder, the most beloved dried chile of Mexico because of its lovely sweetness. It is often used in combination with other dried chiles to mellow their sharpness. Ancho is readily available in the Latin section of your supermarket. You can substitute red chile powder in combination with ancho chile powder for the chili powder blend in any of my chili recipes to play with the flavor balance.

The best way to obtain regional New Mexican chile powders is by mail order. You can order Dixon or Chimayo chile powders from The Chile Shop, 109 East Water Street, Santa Fe, New Mexico, 87501 (505-983-6080, www.thechileshop.com). A ½-pound bag costs around $5. Keep it in a tightly sealed glass jar to preserve its freshness.

The traditional thickener for chili is masa harina, the flour used to make tortillas. It is finely ground cornmeal made from lime-treated dried hominy. The most visible and seemingly logical first choice when looking for masa harina, either in the supermarket or in a Latin grocery, is the big 5-pound paper bag from Quaker or Maseca (packaged in Mexico). But to buy such a big bag is not what I consider practical for using a few tablespoons now and then to thicken a small pot of chili. So I suggest a smaller bag if you can find one.

Jacquie also turned me on to fresh masa harina for tortillas (there is another, coarser grind for tamales) from the Santa Fe School of Cooking pantry retail shop. You may contact them at 116 West San Francisco Street, Santa Fe, New Mexico, 87501 (505-983-4511, www.santafeschoolofcooking.com). They will not give out their source for the most delicious masa harina in the world, but Jacquie and I figure it is from one of the pueblos in Mexico. Mail order a 1-pound bag and keep it in your freezer for up to a year.

Texas Chili

Texas chili is the original beef chili in a world of thousands, maybe hundreds of thousands, of chili stew variations. No beans, no onions, no tomatoes—it is almost naked in its intense, spicy glory. It calls for an extra-coarse grind of chuck known as "chili grind," the most flavorful ground beef in my opinion, so you won't end up with a pot of sloppy Joes. A good butcher will grind it for you if you cannot find it in your supermarket case, or else you can grind your own in a grinder attachment to a KitchenAid stand mixer or in a food processor. I also recommend getting some pure New Mexico red chile powder (see page 55), an important flavor in the chili, and fresh masa harina, the limey cornmeal used to make tortillas. Surprisingly, you control the heat with the cayenne, not the dried pulverized red chiles. Thanks to Elaine Corn, who grew up in the border town of El Paso, Texas, and her groundbreaking, award-winning book *Now You're Cooking* (Harlow & Ratner, 1994) for being the guide for this dish, as well as a great friend. ○ *Serves 2*

COOKER: 1½ or 3 quart
SETTINGS AND COOK TIMES: HIGH for 1 hour, then LOW for 6 to 7 hours, then HIGH for 15 minutes; masa harina added during last 15 minutes

1 pound beef chuck, coarsely ground (chili grind)
2 cloves garlic, finely chopped
2 tablespoons New Mexican red chile powder
2½ teaspoons crumbled dried oregano, preferably Mexican
2½ teaspoons ground cumin
¼ to ½ teaspoon cayenne pepper, to your taste
½ to 1 teaspoon salt, to your taste
2 tablespoons masa harina
3 tablespoons cold water
Shredded Longhorn cheese for serving
Diced red onion for serving
Fresh jalapeño chiles or jalapeños *en escabeche,* chopped, for serving
Whole wheat saltines for serving

1. In a medium-size heavy skillet over medium-high heat, brown the meat until no longer pink and the natural juices boil away; drain off the fat. Add the garlic, chile powder, oregano, cumin, and cayenne pepper to the skillet and cook for 30 seconds. Scrape into the slow cooker. Add water to come up to an even level with the top of the meat. Cover and cook on HIGH for 1 hour.

2. Adjust the heat to LOW and cook for another 6 to 7 hours. Stir twice during the cooking time. At the end of the cooking time, add the salt.

3. In a small bowl, whisk together the masa harina with the cold water to make a paste; stir into the chili, cover, and turn the heat back to HIGH. Cook until the chili thickens, another 15 minutes.

4. Serve hot, with the cheese, red onion, and chiles in small bowls and the saltines on the side.

Stevie's Poker Night Chili

L eave it to my friend Stevie Yvaska to design a unique, assertive chili for the guys. This recipe uses the premixed meatloaf mix available at the meat counter, three types of canned beans, and a package of McCormick's flavorful chili spice mixture for ease. It makes enough for four big bowls. Says Stevie, "You want leftovers with this recipe!" ○ *Serves 2 with leftovers*

COOKER: 3 quart
SETTING AND COOK TIME: HIGH for 3 to 4 hours

1 pound meatloaf mix (ground veal, pork, and beef)
½ red onion, finely chopped
2 cloves garlic, minced
One 15-ounce can Great Northern beans, rinsed and drained
One 15-ounce can red kidney beans, rinsed and drained
One 15-ounce can garbanzo beans, rinsed and drained
Two 14.5-ounce cans stewed tomatoes (Cajun or Italian style), undrained
½ teaspoon chili powder
½ teaspoon celery seed, crushed in a mortar and pestle
One 1-ounce envelope chili seasoning
Tortilla chips for serving
Shredded sharp cheddar cheese for serving

1. In a large skillet over medium-high heat, cook the meat, onion, and garlic until the meat is browned; drain off any fat. Place in the slow cooker and add all the beans, undrained tomatoes, chili powder, celery seed, and chili seasoning package. Stir to combine. Cover and cook on HIGH for 3 to 4 hours. (You can turn the cooker to LOW at any time and let it cook longer, as the longer you let it simmer, the better it gets.)

2. Place a handful of tortilla chips in each serving bowl, then ladle the chili over them and top with the cheese. Serve immediately.

In-a-Pinch Black Bean Chili

his is a quick-in-the-crock chili made with canned black beans, one of the tastiest of all canned beans. It has a jar or two of chunky salsa added, and it is ever so good. In addition to its other virtues, this chili freezes well.

○ *Serves 2 with leftovers*

COOKER: 3 quart
SETTING AND COOK TIME: HIGH for 2½ to 3 hours

2 tablespoons olive oil
1 medium-size onion, chopped
½ teaspoon ground cumin
¼ teaspoon chili powder or 1 teaspoon chipotle chile paste (see page 119)
Two 15-ounce cans black beans, undrained
½ cup chicken broth or vegetable broth, canned or homemade (see page 17 or 18)
1½ cups medium or hot chunky salsa
Pinch of crumbled dried marjoram
Juice and grated zest of 1 lime
Plain yogurt or sour cream (optional) for serving
Chopped cilantro for serving
Saltine crackers or flour tortillas (optional) for serving

1. In a small sauté pan, heat the oil over medium heat and cook the onion until limp. Add the cumin and chili powder, and stir to heat.

2. Pour the beans and their liquid, chicken broth, salsa, and the spicy cooked onions into the slow cooker. Cover and cook on HIGH for 2½ to 3 hours.

3. At the end of the cooking time, stir in the marjoram, lime juice, and lime zest. Serve the chili in bowls, topped with a spoonful of yogurt, if desired, lots of cilantro, and some crackers or warm tortillas, if desired.

Vegetable Chili con Carne

his is adapted from a creative Jane Brody recipe from the *Good Food Book* (W.W. Norton & Co., 1985). It is a chili with ground meat, a little bit of beans, and lots of chunky vegetables like chayote squash, sweet potato, and corn. I adapted it for the slow cooker and made a few changes, but it is essentially the quintessential modern-day chili for people who want to eat a lot of vegetables along with their meat and beans. I vary the recipe with appaloosa, rattlesnake, or anazasi beans, if I can find them at the health food store. You can multiply this recipe as many times as you want in case of a celebration, using a larger slow cooker, of course. I like to serve this with a dollop of plain yogurt, chopped plum tomatoes, shredded cilantro, and warm Hot Pepper Cornbread (page 229).

o *Serves 2*

COOKER: 3 quart

SETTING AND COOK TIME: LOW for 7 to 8 hours

1 tablespoon olive oil

1 small yellow onion, chopped

1 clove garlic, minced

½ pound lean ground beef

One 15.5-ounce can crushed tomatoes in puree, undrained

2½ teaspoons mild chili powder, or to taste

2½ teaspoons brown sugar

1¼ teaspoons ground cumin

1 teaspoon crumbled dried oregano

¼ teaspoon ground coriander

⅛ teaspoon ground allspice

Pinch of ground cloves

1 small jalapeño chile, stemmed, seeded, and minced

½ green bell pepper, diced

½ medium-size carrot, diced

½ chayote squash, peeled, seeded, and diced

1 small sweet potato, peeled and diced

2 stalks celery, chopped
One 15-ounce can pinto beans, rinsed and drained
½ cup fresh or thawed frozen corn kernels
Salt to taste

1. In a large skillet over medium-high heat, heat the olive oil and cook the onion and garlic until limp, about 1 minute. Add the ground beef and cook until the meat is browned; dab with a paper towel to soak up extra fat, if necessary. Place in the slow cooker and add the undrained tomatoes, chili powder, brown sugar, all the spices, the jalapeño, green pepper, carrot, chayote, sweet potato, and celery. Stir to combine. Cover and cook on LOW for 3½ hours.

2. Uncover and add the beans, corn, and salt. Stir to combine. Re-cover and cook another 3½ to 4 hours on LOW, until all the vegetables are tender. Serve hot.

Freezing Fresh Herbs

Freezing herbs is an excellent way to use up the leftover herbs when you buy a fresh bunch and use only a few tablespoons. For a close-to-fresh flavor, wash and dry the leaves and strip them from the stems. Chop or leave whole, as desired. Place in small plastic freezer bags and freeze for up to 3 months. Break off portions to use as needed. The herbs can be used frozen or defrosted, but must be used as soon as possible. Do not refreeze. This method is especially good for mint, cilantro, basil, sage, marjoram, epazote, and chives.

Heating Tortillas

If you serve tortillas with your chili, you will want 1 to 3 corn tortillas per person, or 1 to 2 flour tortillas per person.

In the oven: Heat the oven to 400°F. Place individual corn or flour tortillas directly on the rack and bake 2 to 3 minutes, or until soft and pliable. Or wrap stacks of 4 in aluminum foil or place in a terra cotta tortilla warmer, and heat at 350°F for about 15 minutes.

On a cast-iron skillet or griddle: Heat an ungreased pan over medium-high heat until hot. Place a corn or flour tortilla on the surface and heat until just puffy, about 10 seconds. Turn once. Use a tablespoon of oil if a crispy tortilla is desired.

On a stovetop grill or grill: Heat a gas grill or charcoal fire to medium-high heat. Place a corn or flour tortilla on the grill and heat until just puffy, turning once.

In a microwave oven: Place corn or flour tortillas in a single layer on the microwave tray and warm until just puffy, about 30 seconds. Be careful, as tortillas overbaked in the microwave are very tough. Or wrap stacks in waxed paper and microwave at 2-minute intervals, or until the stack is warm and pliable.

In a bamboo steamer: Wrap a stack of corn or flour tortillas in a clean dish towel and place in a vegetable steamer basket over an inch of boiling water. Cover and steam for 5 to 8 minutes, or until the stack is warm and pliable.

Quick Hominy and Zucchini Chili

This chili is simply a combination of canned hominy, tomatoes, and fresh zucchini, and it is so very good. You are going for an equal proportion of squash and hominy here. It is a delightfully chunky vegetarian chili and has a mild degree of heat, so you can serve it to all manner of diners (add a sprinkling of cayenne pepper if you want more heat). Accompanied by warm tortillas and maybe a sausage or some cold chicken, this makes a nice lunch dish. I like to serve it with sharp cheddar cheese, which counterpoints the sweetness of the chili, plenty of the lime sour cream, and a side of corn chips. ○ *Serves 2*

COOKER: 1½ quart
SETTING AND COOK TIME: HIGH for about 2½ hours

⅔ cup chopped tomatoes, undrained
One 15-ounce can white hominy, rinsed and drained
2 medium-size zucchini, cut into 1-inch chunks
A few shakes of garlic powder
1 teaspoon olive oil
1 medium-size white boiling onion or shallot, finely chopped
1 stalk celery, chopped
1¼ teaspoons chili powder of your choice
Salt to taste
Juice and zest of 1 lime
⅓ cup sour cream mixed with the zest of 2 small limes, for serving
⅔ cup shredded white cheddar cheese for serving
1 green onion, chopped, for serving
Chopped cilantro for serving

1. Add the tomatoes and their juice, hominy, zucchini, and a few shakes of garlic powder to the slow cooker.

2. Heat the oil in a small skillet and cook the onion and celery a bit, just to soften. Add the chili powder and blend with the vegetables, then add the mixture to the crock. Stir to combine. Cover and cook on HIGH for about 2½ hours.

3. Season with salt and stir in the lime juice and zest. Serve in bowls, topped with a spoonful each of lime sour cream, cheese, green onion, and cilantro.

•• Fresh Beans for Your Chili from the Slow Cooker ••

The chili recipes in this chapter all call for canned beans. What if you want to take advantage of your little slow cooker and make a small portion of beans fresh from scratch? No problem.

I used to struggle to get a good pot of plain beans until I started using the slow cooker to cook them. Follow a few guidelines and all dried beans can be fully and beautifully cooked in just a few hours. Unlike on the stovetop, there is almost no risk of burning your beans, as long as you take care to make sure they are always covered with water. This water will turn into what is called the bean liquor, and if you are refrigerating the beans after cooking them, they should be stored in their liquor. Be careful not to overcook, as beans can get mushy in the slow cooker (though they will still be good to eat). Yellow split peas and garbanzo beans are the exception; they remain shapely no matter how long they are cooked. Always check your beans toward the end of the cooking time and add more boiling water if they look too dry. If the beans are to be used in another dish, such as chili, soup, vegetable stew, or a cassoulet, you will want to cook them *al dente* rather than allowing them to become totally soft.

The white varieties of beans, all very different in appearance, include garbanzos, navy beans, baby white beans, Great Northerns, black-eyed peas, yellow-eyed peas, soybeans, and cannellini. These all take about 3 hours to cook in the slow cooker, except for garbanzos and soybeans, which take about 4 hours.

The rose-pink to red-black varieties include black beans (*frijoles negros,* or turtle beans), pintos (nicknamed the Mexican strawberry because of their mottled coloring) and their hybrids (such as rattlesnake and appaloosa beans), red kidneys, small pink beans, anasazi beans, red beans, Jacob's cattle beans, and cranberry beans (also called borlotti or brown beans). These all take about 3 hours to cook.

You can cook the beans completely plain, or flavor them by adding a *bouquet garni,* a single fresh or dried chile pepper, or a sprig or two of fresh herbs. Add hot water (very hot to boiling) to the dried beans, then cover and cook on the HIGH heat setting. Do not add salt until *after* the beans are cooked; salt added at the beginning toughens beans and prevents them from absorbing water properly during the cooking process. Remember that beans and legumes always take slightly longer to cook at higher altitudes.

You can use cooked-from-scratch or canned beans in any of my recipes. Want to substitute your fresh beans for canned? Here are the guidelines: A 15-ounce can of beans, drained, contains about 1½ cups of beans. A 16-ounce can of beans, drained, contains about 1¾ cups of beans. A 19-ounce can of beans, drained, contains about 2 cups of beans. One pound of raw dried beans (approximately 2⅓ cups) will yield about 5 cups of cooked beans.

Basic Slow Cooker Beans ○ ½ cup of dried beans yields 1 to 1½ cups of cooked beans; ¾ cup of dried beans yields 1¾ to 2¼ cups of cooked beans; 1 cup of dried beans yields 2½ to 3 cups of cooked beans

The three ingredient options below reflect different amounts of finished cooked beans; the cooking instructions are the same regardless of the amount of beans you decide to make. The final yield will vary slightly depending on the size and age of the beans you choose to cook.

COOKER: 1½ or 3 quart
SETTING AND COOK TIME: HIGH for 3 to 4 hours

½ cup dried beans
2½ cups boiling water

¾ cup dried beans
3¼ cups boiling water

1 cup dried beans
4 cups boiling water

Salt to taste (optional)

1. Place the beans in a colander and rinse under running water; pick over for small stones. Place in the slow cooker.

2. Add the boiling water to the beans in the crock. Cover and cook on HIGH until tender, 3 to 4 hours. The beans should still hold their shape and not be falling apart, and most of the cooking liquid will be absorbed. I test the beans at 2½ hours by biting into one. Add more boiling water during the cooking if the beans start to look too dry. Add salt if desired. Drain and proceed with your recipe, or store the beans, in their liquid, in the refrigerator for up to 2 days. Drain before using.

Slow Cooker Turkey Chili Mac

Some people just go crazy for chili mac. You can leave out the corn and olives if you like it plain, but they make this chili really tasty. Use really good-quality chili and chile powders for this. ● *Serves 2 with leftovers*

COOKER: 3 quart
SETTING AND COOK TIME: LOW for 5 to 5½ hours; pasta, corn, and olives added after 4 hours

1 tablespoon olive oil
1 small yellow onion, finely chopped
1 clove garlic, minced
1 pound ground dark turkey
One 14.5-ounce can diced tomatoes, drained
2½ teaspoons chili powder
½ teaspoon ancho chile powder
Pinch of ground cumin
Pinch of crumbled dried marjoram
½ teaspoon salt
½ pound elbow macaroni, baby shells, or mini penne tubes, parcooked and drained
½ cup frozen baby white corn, thawed
One 2-ounce can sliced black olives, drained
1 to 2 cups grated cheddar cheese
¼ cup chopped fresh cilantro for serving

1. Spray the inside of the crock with nonstick cooking spray or grease with olive oil. In a medium-size skillet, heat the oil over medium-high heat and cook the onions and garlic until soft. Stir in the ground turkey and cook until the turkey is cooked through, stirring occasionally to break it up. Drain the fat and place the mixture in the slow cooker.

2. Add the tomatoes, chili powder, ancho chile powder, cumin, marjoram, and salt to the crock; stir to combine. Cover and cook on LOW for 4 hours.

3. Stir the cooked pasta, corn, and olives into the chili. Cover and cook on LOW for another 1 to 1½ hours.

4. Top with the cheese to let it melt, and serve out of the crock. Sprinkle each bowl of chili with cilantro.

Grains, Pasta Casseroles, and Sauces

You might be surprised to learn that pasta, polenta, risotto, and even oatmeal can be made in a slow cooker, but they most definitely can. And you'll be amazed at how wonderfully the slow cooker makes oatmeal overnight while you sleep. This rich chapter of slow cooker meals will delight you with their ingenuity, ease of preparation, and economy.

The slow cooker does a glorious job of making some of the fluffiest and most delectable creamy polenta without you having to stand and stir for 30 minutes to an hour. Make a braised beef or chicken cacciatore in one cooker and at the same time make the polenta in another. Fantastic! While polenta is a special coarse grind of dried cornmeal, you can make polenta from regular medium-grind yellow cornmeal. In northeastern Italy, they make it with white cornmeal as well.

Risotto is known as a time-consuming dish to make because of all the stirring. Who has time to stand for 30 solid minutes at the stove with wooden spoon in hand? You can make really fabulous risotto in the slow cooker, which allows it to be braised at a gentle, steady, low boil with no stirring. The only important technique to note is that the time frame for cooking must be strictly adhered to, as the risotto can easily be overcooked.

Risotto is made with a very specific type of rounded short-grain rice that cooks up a bit sticky because of its high starch content. It is called Arborio rice, and the best is grown in northern Italy, in the Po River valley. Arborio rice is labeled Fino or Supra Fino and is the right choice for risotto. Lundberg Family Farms of California sells a domestic California Arborio that is giving Italian Arborio some competition, Rice Select sells a Texas Arborio, and CalRiso is a hybrid of Italian and California rice varieties; all can be substituted cup for cup for their imported Italian cousins. There are two other Italian rices grown for risotto that are becoming more mainstream outside of Italy—Carnaroli and Vialone nano. Carnaroli is grown alongside Arborio in Piedmont and Lombardy. In Venice and Verona, Vialone nano is the rice of choice for risotto and is cooked until *all'onde,* or "wavy," which is a bit looser in texture than other risottos; it is readily available now through Williams-Sonoma. You can use all of these types of rices interchangeably in the following risotto recipes, and I encourage you to try them.

Pasta is pure Italian. Traditionally baked pasta dishes do well when translated to the slow cooker. There is also a whole family of pasta sauces, of which I offer you a nice range here. While I love jarred sauces for quick meals, there is nothing like a homemade tomato sauce. Longer-cooked sauces develop a subtle and concentrated flavor. The shorter-cooked sauces, which cook for about 2 hours, are vivid and still fresh. Thick or thin, with or without meat, with or without wine— I hope you try them all.

Basic Polenta

M aking polenta has never been this simple. Here is a basic, all-purpose recipe. Polenta by itself is bland, so it likes to be dressed up with toppings of cheese, herbs, or a sauce. Or serve it as a bed for a stew or braised meat dish with lots of sauce. I love it plain, using a mixture of Parmesan and fontina cheeses. This recipe makes a soft, fluffy polenta; see the variation below for a firmer, pan-fried version. ● *Serves 2*

COOKER: 1½ to 3 quart
SETTINGS AND COOK TIMES: HIGH for 30 minutes, then LOW for 4 to 5 hours

2½ cups water
½ cup coarse-grain yellow polenta or cornmeal
½ teaspoon salt
2½ tablespoons unsalted butter
⅓ cup grated or shredded Parmesan or Italian fontina cheese

1. Place the water, polenta, and salt in the slow cooker. With a whisk, stir for a few seconds. Cover and cook on HIGH for 30 minutes to heat the water.

2. Stir again, turn the heat to LOW, and cook for 4 hours, stirring occasionally with a wooden spoon. The polenta will thicken quite quickly after 2 hours, expanding magically in the cooker and looking done, but it will need the extra time to cook all the grains evenly. At 4 hours, taste to make sure the desired consistency has been reached and all the grains are tender. You can cook 30 to 60 minutes longer, if you like; the longer the polenta cooks, the creamier it will become. When done, it will be smooth and pull away from the sides of the crock, will be very thick yet pourable, and a wooden spoon will stand up by itself without falling over (the true Italian test). Polenta will be fine on the LOW or KEEP WARM setting for an additional hour, if necessary; add a bit more hot water if it gets too stiff. Stir before serving.

3. To serve as a mound of soft polenta, portion out with an oversized spoon onto a plate or shallow soup bowl. Top with a pat of butter and sprinkle with cheese. Serve immediately.

Saffron Polenta: Add a pinch of saffron threads to the water and polenta at the beginning of cooking. Cook as directed. This is good with all Italian-style meat dishes with tomato, like Spicy Chicken Cacciatore with Fennel Seed and Balsamic Vinegar (page 107) or Pork Stew Peperonata (page 143).

Fried Polenta with Herbs: Prepare the polenta with 2 cups water instead of 2½ cups water, to make a firmer mush. Cook as directed. Line a 6 × 3-inch loaf pan with plastic wrap. After cooking, stir in the Parmesan; 1 teaspoon chopped fresh sage, basil, or rosemary; and 1 tablespoon butter. Pour into the pan, smooth out the top, cover with plastic wrap, and refrigerate overnight. Unmold on a cutting board, cut into thick slices, and fry in a hot skillet with olive oil until both sides are crisp and golden. Serve with hot marinara sauce ladled over the top or on the side, if you like.

Vegetable Polenta with Mascarpone Cheese

(M)ascarpone is an Italian cream cheese that is to-die-for good. It is usually served sweetened in the famous dessert tiramisu, but many areas of Italy use it as a savory ingredient as well. Here it is stirred into the polenta at the end, and it is one of the best ways to enjoy this buttery, rich treat. Use leftover vegetables if you can, to speed the preparation. Thanks to Joyce Goldstein for this inspiration. ○ *Serves 2*

COOKER: 1½ to 3 quart
SETTINGS AND COOK TIMES: HIGH for 30 minutes, then LOW for 4 to 5 hours

2½ cups water
½ cup coarse-grain yellow polenta or cornmeal
½ teaspoon salt
¾ cup coarsely chopped cooked broccoli, spinach, Swiss chard, or zucchini, or mashed cooked
   winter squash
½ cup steamed fresh English peas or thawed frozen petit peas
¼ cup mascarpone cheese
2 tablespoons grated Parmigiano-Reggiano cheese

1. Place the water, polenta, and salt in the slow cooker. With a whisk, stir for a few seconds. Cover and cook on HIGH for 30 minutes to heat the water.

2. Stir again, turn the heat to LOW, and cook for 4 hours, stirring occasionally with a wooden spoon. At 4 hours, taste to make sure the desired consistency has been reached and all the grains are tender. You can cook for 30 to 60 minutes longer, if you like; the longer the polenta cooks, the creamier it will become. When done, it will be smooth and pull away from the sides of the crock, will be very thick yet pourable, and a wooden spoon will stand up by itself without falling over.

3. Stir in the vegetables and mascarpone cheese. Portion out with an oversized spoon onto a plate or shallow soup bowl. Sprinkle with the Parmigiano-Reggiano cheese and serve immediately.

•• Slow Cooker Risotto Basics ••

There are three distinct steps to making perfect risotto in the slow cooker that are similar to making a rice pilaf: cooking the onion and rice, adding the stock and other ingredients, and adding the butter and cheese to finish, known as creaming.

1. Risotto is made by first sautéing chopped onion, then the rice, in butter (or half butter and half olive oil). Place the butter, in pieces, in a sauté pan over medium-high heat. Butter as the cooking fat is traditional for sautéing the onion, but these days a bit of olive oil can be added, or maybe some pancetta. Add chopped onion, leek, or shallot to the pan; cook until soft and any exuded liquid evaporates. If using wine, add and cook for a minute or so. Add the measured amount of rice to the hot butter and onion; stir with a wooden spoon. The rice will gradually heat up and gently sizzle. Stir occasionally and gently to coat all the grains. Give the rice a full 1 to 2 minutes to cook. This precooks the outer coating of the rice to keep the grains separate.

2. Scrape the hot rice mixture into the slow cooker with a heatproof rubber spatula. Add the stock (never water) all at once, and any other ingredients as specified in the recipe. Stir a few times. Cover and cook on HIGH. You may open the slow cooker once or twice during cooking to stir gently, but this is optional. You will have 3 to 4 times as much liquid as rice, and there will be less evaporation with the cover closed than when you cook it on the stovetop. Never add wine at the end; it will taste too bitter and the alcohol will not be cooked off, affecting the delicate taste of your risotto.

3. Check the rice for tenderness at 2 hours, and either continue cooking as necessary or turn off the machine. With a plastic or wooden spoon, stir the risotto a few times, adding the butter and cheese or cream. The bit of butter swirled in at the end of cooking is very traditional but optional. Risotto is best served immediately (it thickens dramatically as it stands at room temperature), but in a pinch will keep on the KEEP WARM setting for up to an hour. A warm shallow soup bowl is nice for serving, along with a soup spoon, but correct risotto etiquette dictates the use of a fork, with more Parmesan cheese for sprinkling (use as much as you like) and the pepper grinder close by.

Lynn's Springtime Risotto for Two

Making risotto in the slow cooker is a snap!" says Lynn Alley, author of three slow cooker books of her own. "Although you could include any number of delicious, tender spring veggies, such as baby artichokes or young carrots, I've simply used tender asparagus tips and peas." ● *Serves 2*

COOKER: 1½ quart
SETTING AND COOK TIME: HIGH for 2 to 2½ hours

1 tablespoon olive oil
3 tablespoons finely chopped onion
2 cloves garlic, finely minced
1 cup Arborio rice
½ cup dry white wine
3 cups water or chicken broth or light vegetable broth, canned or homemade (see page 17 or 18)
½ cup thawed frozen petit peas or garden peas
½ cup fresh or thawed frozen asparagus tips
¼ cup grated Parmigiano-Reggiano cheese
2 tablespoons unsalted butter
Salt and freshly ground black pepper to taste

1. In a small sauté pan over medium heat, warm the oil. Cook the onion until soft, 3 minutes. Add the garlic and rice and cook for 1 minute, stirring. Add the wine and cook, uncovered, until reduced by half, about 8 minutes. Scrape the mixture into the slow cooker with a heatproof rubber spatula. Add the broth, peas, and asparagus tips.

2. Cover and cook on HIGH for 2 to 2½ hours. The risotto should be only a bit liquid, and the rice should be *al dente,* tender with just a touch of tooth resistance. Add butter. Re-cover and wait a minute for the butter to soften. Stir in the cheese and season with the salt and pepper. Serve immediately, spooned into bowls.

Risotto with Pancetta and Potatoes

his is an irresistible recipe, an unexpected combination geared toward potato lovers and especially satisfying for hearty winter appetites. It is adapted from *With the Grain,* a fabulously original cookbook by Raymond Sokolov (Knopf, 1995), who is best known for his 20 years of erudite food commentaries in *Natural History* magazine. As he notes therein about risotto, "It is essential you acquire the appropriate rice"—he recommends Arborio and Carnaroli, along with Vialone nano, the little-known-outside-of-Italy Maratelli, and Spanish paella rice. He also says, "The risotto idea can encompass any ingredient," and encourages you to be inventive when styling your own risotto. Finally, he comments, "Reheated risotto is baneful." Enough said. Eat your fill, leaving not a grain behind. ○ *Serves 2*

COOKER: 1½ quart
SETTING AND COOK TIME: HIGH for 2 to 2½ hours

2 medium-size russet potatoes, peeled and diced
1 tablespoon unsalted butter
1 small onion, finely chopped
1 to 2 slices pancetta, diced
1 cup Arborio, Vialone nano, or Carnaroli rice
3 cups chicken broth, canned or homemade (see page 17)
Pinch of salt
2 tablespoons chopped fresh Italian parsley
⅓ cup grated Parmigiano-Reggiano cheese, plus plenty more for sprinkling

1. Place the potatoes in a colander and rinse with cold water; let drain. In a small sauté pan over medium-high heat, warm the butter. Cook the onion and pancetta until soft and translucent; do not brown. Lower the heat to medium and add the potatoes; cook for 10 minutes, stirring to coat all sides of the potatoes and prevent sticking. Add the rice and cook for another minute, stirring, to coat the grains. Scrape the mixture into the slow cooker with a heatproof rubber spatula. Add the broth and salt.

2. Cover and cook on HIGH for 2 to 2½ hours, until all the liquid is absorbed but the rice is still moist and the potatoes have softened to a mashed consistency. Stir in the parsley and the cheese. Serve immediately, spooned into bowls with more cheese sprinkled on top.

Red Wine Risotto with Mushrooms

(T)his risotto dish uses red wine, which tints the rice pink. This is a prestigious, rich risotto, described by many diners as "robust," and it's quite addictive. ◦ *Serves 2*

COOKER: 1½ quart
SETTING AND COOK TIME: HIGH for 2 to 2½ hours

2½ tablespoons unsalted butter
¼ cup finely chopped onion or 2 shallots, minced
1 small clove garlic, minced
4 ounces fresh mushrooms, halved or thickly sliced depending on size
1 cup Arborio, Vialone nano, or Carnaroli rice
2½ cups chicken broth, canned or homemade (see page 17)
½ cup full-bodied red wine, such as Chianti or Merlot
¼ teaspoon salt
⅓ cup grated or shaved Parmigiano-Reggiano cheese

1. In a small sauté pan over medium heat, melt 1½ tablespoons of the butter. Add the onion, garlic, and mushrooms and cook until soft, 2 minutes. Add the rice and cook for 1 minute, stirring, to coat the grains. Scrape the mixture into the slow cooker with a heatproof rubber spatula. Add the broth, wine, and salt.

2. Cover and cook on HIGH for 2 to 2½ hours, until all the liquid is absorbed but the rice is still moist. Stir in the remaining 1 tablespoon of butter. Sprinkle with the cheese and serve immediately.

• • Slow Cooker Tip: Crockery Care • •

Get in the habit of spraying the inside of the crock with nonstick cooking spray before every recipe to prevent sticking and to facilitate easy washing of the crock. I usually use either a vegetable or an olive oil spray.

Saffron Risotto

isotto with saffron, or *risotto alla milanese,* a specialty of the city of Milan, is one of the trademark dishes of Italian cuisine. It is described in literature as "gilded grains of gold." I recommend using saffron threads instead of powdered saffron, which is really a lot more potent; you want a faint saffron flavor, nothing overstated or overpowering. Vermouth is a fortified dry white wine flavored with herbs and spices. Serve this risotto as a side dish to veal or lamb osso buco, the wonderful Italian braised shanks. Or stir in leftover steamed or roasted vegetables to make a stand-alone dish. ○ *Serves 2*

COOKER: 1½ quart
SETTING AND COOK TIME: HIGH for 2 to 2½ hours

3 cups chicken broth, canned or homemade (see page 17)
½ teaspoon salt
⅛ teaspoon saffron threads, crumbled
1 tablespoon olive oil
2 tablespoons unsalted butter
1 shallot, minced
1 cup Arborio, Vialone nano, or Carnaroli rice
¼ cup dry white vermouth
Freshly ground black pepper to taste
⅓ cup grated Parmigiano-Reggiano cheese

1. In a small saucepan over medium heat, heat 1 cup of the broth with the salt and crush the saffron into it; let stand 15 minutes.

2. In a small sauté pan over medium heat, warm the oil and 1 tablespoon of the butter and add the shallot. Then add the rice and cook, stirring occasionally, for a few minutes, until the rice turns chalky and is coated with the butter. Add the vermouth and cook, uncovered, until most of it is evaporated. Scrape the mixture into the slow cooker with a heatproof rubber spatula. Add the remaining 2 cups broth and saffron broth to the crock.

3. Cover and cook on HIGH for 2 to 2½ hours. The risotto should be only a bit liquid, and the rice should be *al dente,* tender with just a touch of tooth resistance. Season with black pepper. Stir in the remaining 1 tablespoon butter and the cheese. Serve immediately.

Fresh Corn Risotto

(C) orn and rice are a delightful natural pairing. Only make this dish in the summer, when you can use fresh corn cut off the cob. You want one nice-sized ear of corn per person. ● *Serves 2*

COOKER: 1½ quart
SETTING AND COOK TIME: HIGH for 2 to 2½ hours; corn added after 1½ hours

1 tablespoon olive oil
1 large shallot, finely chopped
1 cup Arborio rice
3 cups chicken broth or light vegetable broth, canned or homemade (see page 17 or 18)
2 ears yellow or white corn, shucked and kernels cut off
2 tablespoons unsalted butter
Salt and freshly ground black pepper to taste
¼ cup grated Parmigiano-Reggiano or aged Asiago cheese, plus more for serving
1 plum tomato (optional), seeded and chopped
1 tablespoon minced fresh basil

1. In a small sauté pan over medium heat, warm the oil. Add the shallot and rice and cook, stirring occasionally, for a few minutes, until the rice turns chalky and is coated with the butter. Scrape into the slow cooker with a heatproof rubber spatula. Add the broth.

2. Cover and cook on HIGH for 1½ hours. Stir in the corn and re-cover quickly. Cook for another 30 minutes to 1 hour.

3. The risotto should be only a bit liquid, and the rice should be *al dente,* tender with just a touch of tooth resistance. Add the butter and season with the salt and pepper. Cover and wait a minute for the butter to soften. Stir in the cheese, the tomato, if using, and the basil. Serve immediately, passing additional cheese for sprinkling.

•• Oatmeal in the Slow Cooker ••

Oatmeal made in the slow cooker overnight is creamy, nourishing, and, most important, ready when you are. It is the most heartwarming and nutritious of grains and cooks up thick and luxurious. These recipes, using Scottish or Irish barely processed steel-cut oats or old-fashioned rolled oats, will change your breakfast world; every groat is perfect. Old recipes used to recommend soaking steel-cut oats overnight, since the grains are so tough; that is not necessary with the slow cooker. It works its magic overnight, as slow as can be; lift the lid in the morning and there is your perfectly cooked, creamy oatmeal. No one who makes overnight oatmeal goes back to stovetop preparation—it is that good.

The proportions in these recipes make a moderately thick porridge; if you like it thicker, cut back the water by ½ to 1 cup next time you make it. This is the rib-sticking oatmeal the Scottish eat with a glass of cold ale or stout, or drizzled with single-malt Scotch and brown sugar. We in America like it with a pat of butter, clover honey, and/or light cream.

Remember that your oatmeal is only as good as the kind of oatmeal you get; quick-cooking and instant varieties have no place here.

Overnight Steel-Cut Oatmeal ○ Serves 2

Steel-cut oat nibs, marketed as Irish or Scottish oats, are whole groats that are cut into two or three chunks. This oatmeal is notorious for the long soaking and cooking necessary to soften the oats properly while you wait impatiently for breakfast. No more! Serve with milk or cream, and brown sugar or maple syrup.

COOKER: 1½ to 3 quart
SETTING AND COOK TIME: LOW for 8 to 9 hours, or HIGH for 3 to 4 hours

¾ **cup steel-cut oats**
3 cups water

1. Combine the oats and water in the slow cooker. Cover and cook on LOW for 8 to 9 hours (or on HIGH for 3 to 4 hours), until thick and creamy.

2. Stir well and scoop into serving bowls with an oversized spoon. Serve hot.

(continued)

Steel-Cut Oatmeal with Raisins o Serves 2

Here is another fabulous overnight oatmeal made with steel-cut oats. This one's for the raisin lovers.

COOKER: 1½ to 3 quart
SETTING AND COOK TIME: LOW for 8 to 9 hours, or HIGH for 3 to 4 hours

¾ **cup steel-cut oats**
¼ **cup raisins (or dried cherries, dried blueberries, or dried cranberries)**
Grated zest of 1 orange or tangerine
Pinch of ground mace
3 cups water

1. Combine the oats, raisins, zest, mace, and water in the slow cooker. Cover and cook on LOW for 8 to 9 hours (or on HIGH for 3 to 4 hours), until thick and creamy.

2. Stir well and scoop into serving bowls with an oversized spoon. Serve hot.

Cinnamon-Apple Oatmeal o Serves 2

The combination of apples and oatmeal is one delicious way to have your fruit and grains in the morning. Serve with milk or cream.

COOKER: 1½ quart
SETTING AND COOK TIME: LOW for 8 to 9 hours, or HIGH for 3 to 4 hours

¾ **cup steel-cut oats**
½ **teaspoon apple pie spice, or ground cinnamon with a pinch of cloves, nutmeg, and allspice**
Pinch of salt
3 cups water
4 rings dried apple, chopped
1½ **tablespoons unsalted butter**
2 tablespoons brown sugar

1. Combine the oats, spice, salt, water, and dried apples in the slow cooker. Cover and cook on LOW for 8 to 9 hours (or on HIGH for 3 to 4 hours), until thick and creamy.

2. Stir well, add the butter and sugar, and scoop into serving bowls with an oversized spoon. Serve hot.

Creamy Oatmeal with Lots of Dried Fruit ○ Serves 2

This combination of oatmeal and dried fruit is so popular that the Scots serve it for dessert! Instead of adding more milk when serving, you could serve it simply embellished with a sprinkling of sea salt.

COOKER: 1½ to 3 quart
SETTING AND COOK TIME: LOW for 8 to 9 hours, or HIGH for 3 to 4 hours

¾ **cup steel-cut oats**
¼ **cup chopped dried pears**
¼ **cup chopped dried apricots**
2 **tablespoons currants**
2¾ **cups water**
½ **cup half-and-half, evaporated skim milk, or creamy soymilk, plus more for serving**

1. Combine all the ingredients in the slow cooker. Cover and cook on LOW for 8 to 9 hours (or on HIGH for 3 to 4 hours), until thick and creamy.

2. Stir well and scoop into serving bowls with an oversized spoon. Serve hot, pouring on more milk, if you like.

Old-Fashioned Rolled-Oats Oatmeal ○ Serves 2

This is the recipe in which to use old-fashioned rolled oats or thick-cut rolled oats (not the quick-cooking or instant variety). Serve with mIlk, buttermilk, or cream; a sprinkle of toasted wheat germ; brown sugar; and cinnamon.

COOKER: 1½ to 3 quart
SETTING AND COOK TIME: LOW for 7 to 9 hours, or HIGH for 3 hours

2 **cups old-fashioned rolled oats or thick-cut rolled oats**
4¾ **cups water**
Pinch of salt

1. Combine the oats, water, and salt in the slow cooker; stir to combine. Cover and cook on LOW for 7 to 9 hours (or on HIGH for 3 hours), until thick and creamy.

2. Stir well and scoop into serving bowls with an oversized spoon. Serve hot.

Slow-Baked Macaroni and Cheese

I love old-fashioned pasta tubes in a rich cheesy sauce, and this version, made with fontina cheese, is my favorite. While commercial macaroni and cheese has gotten quite the bad reputation as a convenience food, this Roman rendition will bring the childhood favorite back to your heart with its delicious, satisfying personality. The evaporated milk and egg replace flour as the thickening agent that binds together the oven-baked version. Do not attempt this without the canned milk (you can use skim if you like), as it stabilizes the sauce and prevents it from curdling, which all fresh-milk sauces do in the slow cooker environment. For a special touch, you can sauté some fresh bread crumbs in butter or olive oil and sprinkle them over the top before serving. Serve this with a tossed green salad with tangy vinaigrette and Chianti for a glorious little feast.

● *Serves 2 generously with leftovers*

COOKER: 3 quart
SETTINGS AND COOK TIMES: HIGH for 30 minutes, then LOW for 2 to 2½ hours

1½ cups milk
One 12-ounce can evaporated milk
3 large eggs
¼ cup (½ stick) unsalted butter, melted
½ teaspoon salt
3 cups (12 ounces) shredded Italian fontina cheese
½ pound elbow macaroni or mini penne tubes, parcooked and drained
Freshly ground black pepper to taste
½ cup grated Parmesan cheese

1. Spray the bottom and sides of the inside of the slow cooker with nonstick vegetable spray, or grease with olive oil. Combine the milk, evaporated milk, eggs, butter, and salt in the slow cooker and whisk until smooth, by hand or using an immersion blender. Add the fontina cheese and macaroni, then grind plenty of black pepper over all; gently stir with a rubber spatula to coat evenly. Sprinkle the Parmesan cheese on the top. Cover and cook on HIGH for 30 minutes.

2. Reduce the temperature to LOW and cook for 2 to 2½ hours, until the custard is set in the center and the pasta is tender. The macaroni and cheese may sit in the cooker on the KEEP WARM setting for 30 minutes before serving.

Marinara and Mozzarella Lasagna

Y ou will love this recipe. With two staples from the pantry shelf—dried pasta and a jar of marinara sauce—and some cheese, you can assemble this lasagna in about 5 minutes. A few hours later, you are serving perfect lasagna, right down to the rippled top layer and a dash of golden brown around the edges. The key ingredient is the no-boiling-required lasagna noodles, which are flat rectangles (no ruffled edges); I use Barilla brand, which is a premium dried pasta available nationally. All you do is break up the sheets so they fit in your cooker, and layer the ingredients. The moisture from the sauce in the slow cooker environment is plenty to cook the lasagna noodles perfectly every time. I use whole-milk mozzarella, but you can use any cheese or combination of cheeses you like. Vary the type of sauce, taking advantage of the wealth of delicious sauces available (Classico Cabernet Marinara is a favorite of mine). The $1\frac{1}{2}$-quart cooker makes a lovely dinner for two moderate eaters, with leftovers for another small meal or freezing. You can add a few additional layers if you want a deeper lasagna. ○ *Serves 2 with leftovers*

COOKER: 1 ½ to 3 quart
SETTING AND COOK TIME: HIGH for 3 ½ to 4 hours

Cheese, Please

Italians are sticklers for using the right cheese with their risotto, pasta, and polenta, and I share the sentiment. Buy a chunk of imported Parmigiano-Reggiano, even just a little bit, if you can. You will notice the difference in flavor. You can also use Pecorino Romano, an imported sheep's-milk cheese with a stronger flavor, in place of Parmigiano-Reggiano. It is more reasonably priced. If you choose to buy a domestic Parmesan, try different kinds to find the best quality. You might also use aged Asiago (sometimes called the poor man's Parmesan) or a Parmesan-Romano combination, if you like.

One 26-ounce jar marinara sauce of your choice

5 to 6 sheets no-cook oven-ready lasagna noodles
   (if you are using a 3-quart cooker, you will need 3 more sheets)

½ pound mozzarella cheese, sliced or cubed

¼ cup grated or shredded Parmigiano-Reggiano, Pecorino Romano,
   or aged Asiago cheese

1. Spray the inside of the slow cooker with nonstick cooking spray, or wipe with an olive oil–soaked paper towel. Using a large spoon, spread 2 tablespoons of sauce over the bottom of the crock. Break one pasta sheet into pieces and cover the sauce; it doesn't matter what shape or size the pieces are as long as they fit. Cover with 2 to 3 tablespoons of sauce and a layer of mozzarella cheese. Make 5 to 6 layers total, ending with the marinara sauce. Sprinkle the Parmigiano-Reggiano cheese over the top. The crock will be two-thirds to three-quarters full; the lasagna will collapse as it cooks.

2. Cover and cook on HIGH for 3½ to 4 hours. Test for tenderness by piercing the lasagna with the tip of a sharp knife at 3 to 3½ hours. The lasagna will be fine on the KEEP WARM setting for an additional 2 hours, if necessary. Serve hot, cutting the lasagna with a metal or plastic spatula.

Additions and Variations: If you like, you may add 2 to 3 layers of vegetables, such as cooked or fresh spinach leaves, roasted red peppers, leftover roasted mixed vegetables, thawed frozen or water-packed artichoke hearts, or sautéed mushrooms. The total cook time will increase by 30 minutes to 1 hour, depending on the addition.

Essential Marinara Sauce

Marinara sauce is a quick and easy all-purpose sauce. Load the little slow cooker and let it bubble away. If you want enough to freeze an extra portion, double this recipe. For convenience, use the Italian tomato paste that comes in tubes; it is also a superior-tasting tomato paste to the kind in the can. This sauce is nice made with canned golden tomatoes, if you happen to find them on your supermarket shelf. Flavor this sauce with herbs, Italian style, or the zest of an orange, Provence style, but not both at the same time. Since this is such a light sauce, serve it over angel hair pasta, gemelli twists, mostaccioli (the tubes with no grooves), shells, radiatore, or fusilli. ○ *Makes about 2½ cups*

COOKER: 1½ to 3 quart
SETTING AND COOK TIME: LOW for 4 to 5 hours

3 tablespoons olive oil
1 large shallot, finely chopped
One 28-ounce can whole plum tomatoes, undrained
3 tablespoons tomato paste
2 tablespoons dry red wine or vodka
¼ teaspoon dried mixed Italian herbs or grated zest of 1 orange
Salt and freshly ground black pepper to taste
2 tablespoons unsalted butter or crème fraîche (optional)

1. In a medium-size skillet, heat the olive oil and cook the shallot for 5 minutes to soften. Place the shallot, tomatoes with their juice, tomato paste, wine, and herbs or zest in the slow cooker. Cover and cook on LOW for 4 to 5 hours.

2. Season with salt and pepper. Use a handheld immersion blender to puree the sauce, if desired. Swirl in the butter, if a richer sauce is desired, or the crème fraîche, for a creamy sauce. You can keep the sauce in the cooker on KEEP WARM for a few hours before serving. The sauce will keep in an airtight container in the refrigerator for up to 3 days, or in the freezer for up to 2 months.

My Mom's Fresh Tomato Basil Sauce

This is the sauce to make when fresh tomatoes are in season, and it is brilliant in its simplicity. My mother always makes her sauce year round from fresh tomatoes and keeps portions in the freezer for everything from lasagna and eggplant Parmesan to a single portion of fresh linguine or ravioli. She often makes a batch just because the tomatoes look good, and freezes the whole thing. If you do make a batch for the freezer, do not add the basil to the crock. Instead, add it to the sauce just before serving. Mom uses about $1/4$ cup of basil leaves if flavoring the whole pot. This recipe is so easy because you don't peel or seed the tomatoes, so you can load the crock in minutes. You must put it through a hand food mill, so that simple kitchen tool is crucial to the success of this recipe. Use different olive oils to vary the flavor slightly. **o** *Makes about $3^{1}/_{2}$ cups*

COOKER: 3 quart
SETTING AND COOK TIME: LOW for about 3 hours
(optional to cook on HIGH for first 30 minutes)

2 pounds ripe plum tomatoes, cored and cut into chunks
5 cloves garlic, crushed
$1/4$ to $1/3$ cup extra-virgin olive oil, depending on your mood
Salt and freshly ground black pepper to taste
3 to 4 tablespoons julienned fresh basil leaves

1. Place the tomatoes and garlic in the slow cooker. Pour the olive oil on top. Cover and cook on LOW for about 3 hours, until the tomatoes have broken down into a sauce. (I often cook first on HIGH for 30 minutes to warm the machine up faster.)

2. Over a large bowl, put the sauce through a food mill fitted with the coarse sieve blade. Season with salt and pepper. Place back in the crock and stir in the basil. Cover and allow to cook about 15 minutes longer on HIGH. Serve hot. The sauce keeps in an airtight storage container in the refrigerator for up to 3 days, or in the freezer for up to 2 months.

Sugo di Carne

(T) his is one of my favorite classic Italian sauces. Made with ground veal and pancetta, it is *the* sauce for cheese ravioli. It's also great as an accompaniment to chicken and lamb. This sauce freezes well. If you're freezing it, don't add the fresh basil to the crock; rather, add it to the reheated sauce just before serving.

○ *Makes 2 cups*

COOKER: 1½ to 3 quart
SETTING AND COOK TIME: LOW for 6 to 7 hours

3 tablespoons olive oil
1 small yellow onion, finely chopped
2 slices pancetta or bacon, finely chopped
1 pound ground veal
Salt and freshly ground black pepper to taste
One 14.5-ounce can diced tomatoes, undrained
⅓ cup chicken broth, canned or homemade (see page 17)
5 fresh basil leaves, julienned

1. In a large skillet over medium-high heat, heat the olive oil and cook the onion and pancetta until just beginning to brown, about 5 minutes. Transfer to the slow cooker.

2. Add the veal to the skillet and cook until lightly browned, breaking up the clumps with a spoon. Season with salt and pepper. Add to the slow cooker along with the tomatoes and their juice and the broth. Cover and cook on LOW for 6 to 7 hours.

3. Stir in the basil. Serve the sauce ladled from the crock, or cool the sauce to room temperature, store in airtight containers, and refrigerate for up to 4 days or freeze for up to 1 month.

Italian Tomato Sauce with Cracked Red Pepper and Pancetta

I t was the Italians who developed the art of the sauce, and then it traveled over the Alps to the French court chefs. There is a great variety of sauces for pasta in Italian cuisine, and this tomato sauce, with the cracked red pepper and the Italian fresh bacon called pancetta, is a bit spicy. It is a classic arrabbiata sauce, made "furious" or "angry" with the addition of the hot pepper flakes, and updated for the slow cooker. Serve Neapolitan style, over spaghetti and sprinkled with Parmigiano-Reggiano cheese and fresh Italian parsley, or ladled over a sautéed veal chop. o *Makes 3 ½ cups*

COOKER: 1½ to 3 quart
SETTING AND COOK TIME: LOW for 5 to 6 hours

6 ounces pancetta, chopped
1 medium-size yellow onion, chopped
1 clove garlic, cut into 4 slices
One 28-ounce can diced tomatoes, undrained
3 tablespoons dry red wine, such as Chianti or Zinfandel
½ teaspoon crushed red pepper flakes

1. In a small skillet over medium-high heat, cook the pancetta until the fat is rendered and the meat is crisp, about 8 minutes. Transfer the pancetta to the slow cooker and drain off all but 2 tablespoons of fat from the skillet. Add the onion and garlic to the skillet and cook for 3 minutes, just to soften; add to the crock. Add the tomatoes and their juice and the wine to the crock. Add the red pepper flakes. Cover and cook on LOW for 5 to 6 hours.

2. Serve the sauce hot from the crock, or cool to room temperature, pour into airtight containers, and refrigerate for up to 4 days or freeze for up to 2 months.

Italian Meat Sauce

T his very traditional, long-cooking tomato sauce is made with ground beef or turkey, and it is pure comfort food—thick, rich, and savory. It is good with cheese ravioli, linguine, rigatoni, or penne, but no matter what type of pasta you serve it with, make sure there is plenty of grated Parmigiano-Reggiano cheese, crusty bread, and a nice green salad with fresh tomatoes to serve with it. Since this sauce is so good, even reheated, the recipe yields enough for a second meal. ○ *Makes about 6 cups*

COOKER: 3 quart
SETTING AND COOK TIME: LOW for 6 to 8 hours

2 tablespoons olive oil
2 medium-size yellow onions, diced
1 small carrot, diced
1 stalk celery, diced
1 clove garlic, minced
1 pound lean ground beef or ground turkey
½ cup dry white wine
Salt and freshly ground black pepper to taste
One 35-ounce can whole plum tomatoes with basil, undrained
One 6-ounce can tomato paste

1. In a large skillet over medium-high heat, heat the oil and cook the onions, carrot, and celery until just beginning to brown, about 10 minutes. Add the garlic and cook for 30 seconds. Transfer the vegetables to the slow cooker.

2. Add the beef to the skillet and cook until lightly browned, breaking up the clumps with a spoon. Add the wine and cook, allowing the wine to evaporate a bit; season with salt and pepper. Add the beef and wine to the crock. Add the tomatoes and juices, breaking up the tomatoes with the back of a spoon, and the tomato paste. Cover and cook on LOW for 6 to 8 hours.

3. Serve the sauce ladled from the crock, or cool the sauce to room temperature, store in airtight containers, and refrigerate for up to 4 days or freeze for up to 1 month.

Perennial Favorites
Chicken and Turkey

Chicken braises beautifully in the slow cooker, and a world of flavors beckons—anything goes, from tandoori to Moroccan, Caribbean, Mexican, and Italian; from elegant French to down-home barbecue. Whether bone-in or boneless, breasts, thighs, wings, or drumsticks, chicken is a slow cooker staple.

Poultry pieces cook more efficiently than a whole bird and are especially convenient portions for small-batch cooking. Boneless pieces,

such as breasts and thighs, cook the fastest, with bone-in pieces taking longer. Please add extra time, 1 to 2 hours on LOW, if substituting bone-in poultry for boneless in a recipe, or follow the instructions in a recipe designed for the type of poultry you are using.

A number of my recipes call for boneless chicken breasts, since that is one of the most popular cuts for everyday cooking. Boneless breasts cook the fastest and are best cooked on HIGH for a short time. Boneless duck breasts are surprisingly lean and are prepared in the same manner as chicken breasts. I also use boneless chicken thighs, which have their own velvety texture after braising. But I have been known to make a meal of drumsticks or wings too, so there are recipes here using all parts. Drumsticks and dark thigh meat are best cooked for an extended amount of time on LOW. Wings get cooked on HIGH since they are so spare.

Fresh poultry needs to be stored in the refrigerator until preparation time and cooked within 1 to 2 days after purchase to minimize bacterial growth. Never use room-temperature poultry; it will reach the correct temperature as the slow cooker heats up. Unless a recipe specifically calls for it, never put frozen poultry directly into the slow cooker, since it will take much longer to reach a safe cooking temperature than defrosted refrigerated poultry. Before cooking, rinse the chicken thoroughly with cold water and pat dry. Please note that the danger zone for bacterial growth in poultry is between 40° and 140°F. The heating rate for a slow cooker is 3 to 4 hours on the LOW setting to get the contents up to a safe food temperature of 140° to 165°F; it will then increase to over 200°F by 6 hours. The same temperatures will be reached in half the amount of time on the HIGH setting. Please do not lift the lid for the first 3 to 4 hours, to allow the heat to come to the proper cooking temperature as fast as possible. Many cooks start with an initial hour on HIGH for all their recipes, then lower the temperature, to get the contents cooking faster.

Chicken is done and cooked throughout when the juices run clear and when the internal temperature reaches about 180°F on an instant-read thermometer, an invaluable tool when cooking any meat in the slow cooker. When testing both white and dark meat for doneness, there will be no trace of pink when pierced with the tip of a sharp knife at the thickest point.

No longer relegated just to Thanksgiving, turkey is a meat that is appropriate for any night of the week, any season of the year. Its naturally low fat content and tasty meat have made it a favorite for slow cookery. Stewing and braising turkey parts offers unlimited opportunities for the cook to be creative. By adding your favorite ingredients, herbs, spices, or sauces, it's easy to create unique new dishes. The moist, low heat will pull out the lovely, flavorful juices, which will mix with the cooking liquid to make your sauce or gravy base.

Due to increased demand by cooks, the past 10 years have seen lots more fresh turkey parts and ground meat available. Available fresh or frozen are bone-in or boneless turkey breast halves, boneless breast tenderloins, quartered birds, sliced breast cutlets, thighs and shanks, drumsticks, wings, drumettes, turkey bacon, turkey sausage, and ground turkey. These options are not only economical, but are also much more convenient and faster to cook than a whole bird. Count on 1 pound of bone-in turkey meat per person, and 3/4 pound per person if the meat is boneless. I figure one turkey leg per person, but if the legs are large, you may wish to carve the meat off the bones, in which case one leg will serve two. I always portion one turkey thigh per person. The half turkey breast with the bone in is one of the best meals for two in the slow cooker—put it in and turn on the machine. The slow cooker keeps the lean breast incredibly moist instead of drying it out, as when it is roasted in the oven.

Use all fresh or thawed turkey within 2 to 3 days of purchase. Freeze raw poultry for only about 6 months maximum for the best texture. Refrigerate cooked poultry within 2 hours after serving, never letting it come to room temperature first before refrigerating. Cooked turkey keeps for 3 to 4 months in the freezer. Because turkey, like all poultry, can carry potentially harmful organisms or bacteria, take care when handling. Thoroughly wash and dry it before preparation. Wash your hands, work surfaces, and utensils with hot soapy water before and after handling. Turkey should always be cooked completely through, until an instant-read meat thermometer registers 170° to 180°F, and never eaten raw, or rare like beef and lamb, since the organisms can permeate the meat.

Slow cooking is an excellent method for cooking turkey, and I hope this chapter, which features a variety of turkey parts, will inspire you to cook it at least once a week. And don't forget some cranberry sauce to serve on the side (pages 134–135)!

Salsa Chicken with Cheese

There is a wealth of fabulous jarred salsas on the market today, and I always keep a few in the pantry, since this is one of my favorite recipes. Serve over steamed long-grain brown jasmine rice, or as a sandwich in a hot flour tortilla with some black beans on the side. This tastes great with guacamole as well. ○ *Serves 2*

COOKER: 3 quart
SETTING AND COOK TIME: HIGH for 1½ to 2 hours;
    cheese added during last 10 minutes

2 boneless, skinless chicken breast halves, trimmed of fat
⅔ cup of your favorite medium or hot prepared chunky salsa
Juice of ½ lime or 1 tablespoon dry white wine
2 ounces crumbled goat cheese or 3 slices white cheddar or mozzarella cheese

1. Spray the inside of the crock with nonstick cooking spray, and arrange the chicken breasts in the crock. Pour the salsa over the chicken and drizzle the lime juice over the top. Cover and cook on HIGH for 1½ to 2 hours, until the chicken is tender and cooked through. The chicken will make its own juice as well.

2. Sprinkle or lay the cheese over each breast, cover, and let stand 10 minutes before serving, to melt the cheese. Serve immediately.

Energy Economy

The slow cooker is user-friendly and very economical, using about the same amount of energy as a 75-watt lightbulb. It takes much less electricity to use a slow cooker than a conventional gas or electric oven. It is an excellent alternative method of cooking on extremely hot days when energy alerts recommend reduced use of electrical appliances, and it won't add heat to your kitchen like an oven does.

Moroccan-Spiced Tomato Chicken with Almonds

H ere is a totally different chicken laced with some subtle spices, currants, and honey in a tomato-based sauce that uses cooked salsa. It is a brilliantly simple recipe that tastes like a whole lot more than its parts and is adapted from my friends' favorite recipe from one of the best cookbook series in print, *The Best American Recipes* by Fran McCullough (Houghton Mifflin, 1999). Serve with plain couscous for authenticity. ○ *Serves 2*

COOKER: 1½ to 3 quart
SETTING AND COOK TIME: LOW for 2 to 2½ hours

2 teaspoons olive oil
2 tablespoons slivered almonds
1 clove garlic, minced
4 boneless, skinless chicken thighs
1 cup tomato salsa (I use Salsa de Luna or Newman's Own Mild Chunky)
2 tablespoons dried currants
4 teaspoons honey
¼ teaspoon ground cumin
¼ teaspoon ground cinnamon
Salt and freshly ground black pepper to taste

1. Spray the inside of the crock with nonstick cooking spray. Heat the oil in a large skillet over medium-high heat until hot. Add the almonds and cook, stirring, until golden, 1 minute. Remove from the skillet with a slotted spoon and set aside to drain on paper towels. When cool, coarsely chop.

2. Add the garlic to the skillet and cook, stirring, until just fragrant, about 20 seconds. Add the chicken thighs to the skillet and cook, turning once, until lightly browned, 4 to 5 minutes. Transfer the contents of the skillet to the slow cooker.

3. Combine the salsa, currants, honey, cumin, and cinnamon and pour over the chicken. Cover and cook on LOW for 2 to 2½ hours, until the chicken is fork-tender and the juices run clear when pierced with a fork.

4. Season with salt and pepper. Serve hot, topped with the toasted almonds.

Cashew Chicken Lo Mein

Lo mein is the Eastern Hemisphere's answer to Italian pasta. *Mein* translates to "noodle," and *lo mein* means "mixed noodles." After a short stint in the slow cooker, the vegetables in this recipe stay as crunchy as if they were stir-fried; then they are tossed with the cooked noodles in the crock. Lo mein noodles, also labeled Chinese noodles, are sold fresh in the supermarket produce section. They come thick or thin; you want the thin. Be sure to get the shredded stir-fry vegetables, not the chunks, since they will cook totally differently. Long beans are those extra-long green beans you see in Asian markets. ○ *Serves 2*

COOKER: 3 quart
SETTINGS AND COOK TIMES: LOW for 2 to 2¼ hours, then HIGH for 30 minutes

2 tablespoons sesame oil or olive oil
2 boneless, skinless chicken thighs, trimmed of fat and cut into bite-size pieces
½ medium-size onion, sliced into rings
1 tablespoon minced fresh ginger
¾ cup stir-fry seasoning sauce (such as Kikkoman)
6 to 8 ounces thawed frozen stir-fry vegetables
   (with shredded broccoli, celery, carrots, and pea pods)
4 long beans, cut into 4-inch pieces
1 or 2 heads baby bok choy, chopped (about 2 cups)
¼ cup sliced water chestnuts, drained
2 cups chopped napa cabbage
6 ounces fresh thin Chinese noodles
¼ cup whole roasted cashews
2 tablespoons sliced green onions for serving

1. Spray the inside of the crock with nonstick cooking spray. Heat 1 tablespoon of the oil in a small skillet over medium heat and add the chicken pieces. Stir until the chicken is browned, about 5 minutes. Transfer to the slow cooker. Add the onion and ginger to the crock. Pour in the stir-fry seasoning sauce and stir to coat. Cover and cook on LOW for 2 to $2\frac{1}{4}$ hours, until the chicken is cooked through.

2. When the chicken is done, increase the heat setting to HIGH. Add the stir-fry vegetables, long beans, bok choy, water chestnuts, and cabbage. Cover and cook for 30 minutes, stirring once, or until the vegetables are the desired degree of crisp-tender.

3. Meanwhile, cook the lo mein noodles. Bring a saucepan of lightly salted water to a boil. Fluff the noodles first to loosen the clump and drop into the boiling water. Stir immediately to separate them. Fresh noodles are done in about 1 minute, so stay alert. Drain in a colander, toss with the remaining 1 tablespoon of oil, and set aside until the vegetables are done.

4. Stir the cashews and lo mein noodles into the crock, tossing gently. To serve, portion the hot chicken, vegetable, and noodle mixture onto serving plates (I use tongs and a spoon). Garnish with green onions and serve hot.

Curried Chicken Breasts

The homemade curry paste in this recipe is mild and fabulous and, well, addictive. It is originally from Sujata, who was part of the beloved Indian dance team of Asoka and Sujata, who did bit-part work in Hollywood in the 1940s for exotic dance scenes. Later, after formal retirement, Sujata became a dance teacher in Sedona, Arizona. I have used her curry paste with great success on appetizer chicken wings, but the paste continued to beckon to me from the fridge, so I have tried it here on everyday chicken, and it's wonderful. Make the curry paste before you are ready to make your chicken; it keeps in the refrigerator for weeks. (It makes more than you will need for this chicken, so you can use the leftovers for those chicken wings!) Serve this over basmati rice. ● *Serves 2*

COOKER: 1½ to 3 quart
SETTING AND COOK TIME: HIGH for 2½ to 3 hours

SUJATA'S CURRY PASTE:
2 tablespoons ground coriander
1½ teaspoons ground cumin
1½ teaspoons ground turmeric
¼ teaspoon chili powder
1 teaspoon brown mustard seed, crushed with a mortar and pestle
¼ teaspoon ground cloves
¼ teaspoon ground cardamom
¼ teaspoon ground cinnamon
1½ tablespoons apple cider vinegar
1 to 2 tablespoons water, as needed

1 small yellow or white onion, sliced into rings
2 to 3 boneless, skinless chicken breast halves, trimmed of fat
¼ teaspoon salt
1½ tablespoons Sujata's Curry Paste
1 teaspoon sesame oil or olive oil
¼ cup heavy cream or half-and-half

1. To make the curry paste, combine all of the spices in a small bowl with a fork. Mix in the vinegar, then drizzle in the water to make a loose paste.

2. Spray the inside of the crock with nonstick cooking spray. Place the sliced onion on the bottom for your chicken to sit on. Mix together the curry paste and the oil; rub on the chicken to coat both sides. Place the chicken breasts in the slow cooker and sprinkle with the salt. Cover and cook on HIGH for 2½ to 3 hours.

3. Stir in the heavy cream, and add salt to taste. Serve hot.

·· Slow Cooker Tip: Crockery Care ··

The slow cooker crock can be used in the oven. Just be sure to use aluminum foil to cover it rather than the lid, which is not ovenproof. *Do not* use the slow cooker crock in the microwave or on the stovetop. Do not refrigerate cooked food that is still in the cooker; it will not cool down and chill the contents properly. Always transfer the food to a refrigerator container.

Chicken with Basil Cream Sauce

While most of my slow cooker creations call for ingredients from scratch, here is a departure. A store-bought jar of Alfredo sauce is a wonderful pantry item, letting you throw together a chicken in cream sauce in literally minutes for a very fast entrée. While most dairy cannot be cooked for the entire time in the slow cooker without curdling, the Alfredo sauce is up to the job and makes a luscious, unique sauce melded with the chicken juices. Check out the variations as well; they are all just as wonderful, giving you license to create your own sauce from what you have on hand. I use the 1½-quart slow cooker here, but the 3-quart will work as well. Serve this over pasta or rice, or plain with French bread on the side. ● *Serves 2*

COOKER: 1½ to 3 quart
SETTING AND COOK TIME: HIGH for 2½ to 3 hours

2 boneless, skinless chicken breast halves, trimmed of fat
Salt and freshly ground black pepper to taste
1 cup plain Alfredo sauce (I like Classico brand)
3 to 4 tablespoons Pesto Sauce (recipe follows)

Spray the inside of the crock with nonstick cooking spray, and arrange the chicken breasts in the slow cooker. Sprinkle with salt and pepper. In a small bowl, combine the Alfredo sauce and the pesto sauce; stir to combine, then pour over the chicken. Cover and cook on HIGH for 2½ to 3 hours, until the chicken is tender and cooked through. The chicken will make its own juice and thin the sauce. Serve hot.

Variations
In place of pesto, you could try:

Chicken with Lemon Cream Sauce and Olives: Add 6 to 8 whole black olives (canned or kalamata in brine) and the zest of 1 lemon to the Alfredo sauce.

Chicken with Chipotle Cream Sauce: Add 1 to 1½ tablespoons chipotle paste (see page 119) or ½ mashed chipotle chile and 2 teaspoons of adobo sauce to the Alfredo sauce.

Chicken with Artichoke Cream Sauce: Add ⅔ cup of drained canned or thawed frozen artichoke hearts and 1 tablespoon Marsala wine to the Alfredo sauce.

Chicken with Curry Cream Sauce: Add ½ teaspoon of your favorite mild or hot curry powder (or a dab of Sujata's Curry Paste, page 98) and ½ teaspoon fresh grated ginger to the Alfredo sauce.

Chicken à la King: Add an extra ¼ cup of Alfredo sauce, 2 ounces sliced white or cremini mushrooms, ¼ cup thawed frozen peas, and 1 tablespoon chopped pimiento (drained) to the Alfredo sauce. After cooking, use two forks to shred the chicken into big pieces. Serve over toast cut in half on the diagonal (toast points), waffles, or baked puff pastry shells.

Pesto Sauce

While making your own pesto is by far the best, you can also use a commercial sauce for convenience, if you like. Fresh basil is available year round. Freeze the pesto in portions in little pouches of plastic wrap stored in zipper-top freezer bags or mini plastic freezer containers. ○ *Makes ⅔ cup*

1 small clove garlic
2 tablespoons pine nuts
1 cup fresh basil leaves, firmly packed
1 tablespoon grated Parmesan cheese
⅓ cup olive oil

Combine the garlic and pine nuts in a small food processor and pulse to chop finely. Add the basil and Parmesan cheese; process until a coarse paste. With the machine running, slowly pour the olive oil through the feed tube, processing until it becomes a thick puree flecked with bits of basil. Store in the refrigerator for up to 1 week with a bit of olive oil poured over the top to preserve the color, or freeze for up to 2 months.

Red Curry Chicken Braised in Coconut Milk

hicken braised in coconut milk is a staple in Indonesian and Malay tropical cuisines. I just adore dried mango, and here is a wonderful way to feature it. As it cooks with the savory coconut milk sauce, it will soften and add a luscious sweetness to the cooking juices. Look for the plump, finger-size ripe red chile in the produce bins; it is known in ethnic markets by its Indian name, *lal mirch*. Since it is a ripe version of an immature green chile, the heat will be subdued. Thai red curry paste is a commercially available product and a traditional seasoning in Southeast Asian dishes; it has a completely different taste from Indian curries. Serve this over steamed white or brown jasmine rice.

○ *Serves 2*

COOKER: 1½ to 3 quart
SETTING AND COOK TIME: HIGH for 2½ to 3 hours

1 red chile, seeded
1 tablespoon red curry paste
1 medium-size yellow onion, chopped
One 1½-inch chunk fresh ginger, peeled
1 tablespoon freshly squeezed lime juice
1 tablespoon Asian sesame oil
1 tablespoon low-sodium soy sauce
1 tablespoon honey
Pinch of salt
2 to 3 boneless, skinless chicken breast halves, trimmed of fat
One 13.5-ounce can coconut milk
½ cup chopped dried mango pieces

1. Place the chile, red curry paste, onion, ginger, lime juice, sesame oil, soy sauce, honey, and salt in a food processor and process until smooth to make a loose puree. Scrape into a heavy quart-size zipper-top plastic bag. Add the chicken and mix around to coat completely with the paste. Refrigerate for at least 2 hours or overnight.

2. Place the chicken in the slow cooker. Without shaking it, open the can of coconut milk. Carefully spoon off the top one-third of the liquid in the can (about ½ cup) and add it to the chicken. (The thick portion on top is called the coconut cream; reserve the remaining coconut milk for another purpose.) Stir well to distribute the ingredients and coat the chicken with coconut cream. Add the mango pieces and stir again. Cover and cook on HIGH for to 2½ to 3 hours. Serve hot.

• • Slow Cooker Tip: Lifting the Lid • •

You will see lots of instructions that say never to lift the lid during the cooking process. On one hand, it is a good rule; on the other hand, it is impossible. As the contents of the slow cooker heat up and create steam, a natural water seal is created around the rim of the lid as a vacuum is formed. The rim of the lid will stick in place when gently pulled, and this is important for the even cooking of the food within. But the recipe might call for adding ingredients halfway through cooking or near the end of the cooking time, or you might want to check your food for doneness at some point. It is fine to do this, but always remember that by breaking the lid seal and allowing the steam to escape, the temperature within is reduced. When you place the lid back on, it takes 20 to 30 minutes for the internal temperature of the contents to come back to the proper cooking temperature. You can easily check the contents through the glass lid. There is no need to stir or turn the food, unless a recipe specifies to do so. Otherwise, stirring before serving will suffice.

Chicken Mole

M ole sauce, one of the stalwarts of the Mexican home kitchen, is a combination of russet and dark brown dried chiles, almonds, pumpkin and sesame seeds, spices, stale tortilla pieces, aromatic vegetables, and sometimes even a hint of chocolate. Traditional mole sauce is complex and takes hours even when made in a blender (the original sauce was hand mashed in a stone *metate*), so it was reserved for holidays and celebrations in a dish called *mole poblano de guajolote,* or Mexican wild turkey in mole chile sauce. My friend and Latin food specialist Jacquie Hiquera McMahan says that maybe one in a thousand cooks ever attempts to make mole. With the advent of prepared commercial moles, combined with the slow cooker, this long process is cut to minutes, and I can have an almost completely authentic-tasting mole any time I want. While mole is usually served with turkey in Mexico, chicken, duck, and rabbit are also used; here I use boneless chicken thighs. Serve this over white rice. ◉ *Serves 2*

COOKER: 3 quart
SETTING AND COOK TIME: HIGH for 3 hours, or LOW for 6 hours

1 medium-size yellow or white onion, sliced
4 boneless, skinless chicken thighs
1 teaspoon Mexican seasoning blend
Pinch of salt
1 to 2 tablespoons olive oil
1 large ear corn on the cob (optional), shucked and cut into 4 pieces
½ cup chicken broth, canned or homemade (see page 17)
2 tablespoons prepared mole sauce
    (such as Rogelio Bueno Autentico Mole or Doña Maria brands)
2 tablespoons creamy peanut butter
2 tablespoons dark brown sugar
1 tablespoon chocolate syrup (such as Hershey's)
⅛ teaspoon red pepper flakes
2 teaspoons sesame seeds, toasted in a dry skillet over medium heat
    until golden, for garnish

1. Spray the inside of the crock with nonstick cooking spray and lay the onion in the bottom (it will be the bed for the chicken). Sprinkle the chicken with the Mexican seasoning and the salt.

2. In a medium-size skillet over medium-high heat, warm the oil and add the chicken pieces in a single layer, with the smooth side down. Cook for 2 to 3 minutes, to form a nice browned surface; turn the chicken and brown the second side. Transfer the chicken to the slow cooker, smooth side up. Add the corn sections around the chicken, if using.

3. In a small bowl, combine the chicken broth, mole sauce, peanut butter, brown sugar, chocolate syrup, and red pepper flakes; stir with a fork. Place in the microwave to warm the sauce and melt the peanut butter a little, but don't worry; the sauce will melt together during slow cooking. Pour the mole sauce over the chicken in the crock. Cover and cook on HIGH for 3 hours (or on LOW for 6 hours).

4. Remove the chicken and corn with a large spoon. Serve 2 thighs and 2 pieces of corn per person, sprinkled with the sesame seeds.

Greek Chicken with Feta

This is originally a Lydie Marshall braised chicken recipe, which she got from a friend in Greece, probably decades ago. Then Jane Brody streamlined it in 1985 by using less fat and salt, serving it as a party dish. Now here it is adapted for the little slow cooker. Serve with macaroni or spinach noodles.

○ *Serves 2*

COOKER: 1½ to 3 quart
SETTING AND COOK TIME: LOW for 6 to 8 hours; cheese added during last 15 minutes

One 3-ounce block feta cheese
1 tablespoon olive oil
2 bone-in chicken legs with thighs skinned
1 medium-size yellow onion, thinly sliced
1 clove garlic, minced
Salt and freshly ground black or white pepper to taste
½ of a 14.5-ounce can diced tomatoes, undrained
1 tablespoon tomato paste
Pinch of Greek oregano

1. Place the feta in a bowl with cold water to cover and set aside (this leaches out some of the salt).

2. Heat the olive oil in a medium-size skillet and brown the chicken on both sides. While the chicken is browning, spray the inside of the crock with nonstick cooking spray and lay the onion and garlic in the bottom. Place the browned chicken on top, sprinkle with salt and pepper, and add the tomatoes in juice, tomato paste, and oregano. Cover and cook on LOW for 6 to 8 hours, until the chicken is tender and cooked through.

3. Remove the feta from the water, cut into slices, and arrange the slices over the top of the chicken. Cover and cook for 15 minutes to melt the cheese. Serve immediately.

Spicy Chicken Cacciatore with Fennel Seed and Balsamic Vinegar

C acciatore is southern Italian, and every home cook, as well as restaurant, has a version of *pollo alla cacciatora,* chicken braised with tomatoes and garlic. Here is a delightful version that has a bit of punch with the red pepper flakes and fennel seed. This has plenty of sauce since it is designed to be served over linguine. ○ *Serves 2*

COOKER: 1½ to 3 quart
SETTING AND COOK TIME: HIGH for 4 to 5 hours

2 bone-in chicken breast halves, skin left on
Salt and freshly ground black pepper to taste
1 tablespoon olive oil
One 14.5-ounce can diced tomatoes, undrained
3 tablespoons tomato paste
2 tablespoons dry red wine
1 tablespoon balsamic vinegar
1 to 2 cloves garlic, minced
1 red bell pepper, diced
¼ teaspoon fennel seed
¼ teaspoon crumbled dried marjoram or oregano
¼ teaspoon red pepper flakes

1. Sprinkle the chicken with salt and pepper. Heat the olive oil in a medium-size skillet and brown the chicken on both sides.

2. While the chicken is browning, place the tomatoes in juice, tomato paste, red wine, vinegar, garlic, bell pepper, fennel seed, marjoram, and red pepper flakes in the slow cooker; stir to combine and incorporate the tomato paste.

3. Place the browned chicken in the crock and nestle it into the sauce, spooning the sauce over it. Cover and cook on HIGH for 4 to 5 hours, until the chicken is tender and cooked through. Serve immediately.

Slow-Cooked Pulled Barbecue Chicken

This recipe was contributed by Minneapolis-based food writer and cooking teacher Mary Ellen Evans. "I've taught this in classes and served it to company," she says. "It's always a hit." The secret? A nice little addition of smoky-hot chipotle chile powder. You can double or triple this recipe if you are having company, but don't wait to make this easy and especially tasty casual recipe. Serve with coleslaw and baked beans. ○ *Serves 2*

COOKER: 1½ to 3 quart
SETTING AND COOK TIME: LOW for 7 to 8 hours

1 small white or yellow onion, chopped
1 small clove garlic, minced
4 boneless, skinless chicken thighs
½ cup ketchup
2 tablespoons cider vinegar
2 tablespoons light brown sugar
1 tablespoon olive oil
1½ teaspoons Worcestershire sauce
½ teaspoon chili powder
¼ teaspoon chipotle chile powder
¼ teaspoon salt
2 to 4 soft hamburger buns

1. Sprinkle the onion and garlic over the bottom of the crock and arrange the chicken thighs on top.

2. In a small bowl, stir together the ketchup, cider vinegar, brown sugar, oil, Worcestershire sauce, chili powder, chipotle chile powder, and salt; pour over the thighs. Cover and cook on LOW for 7 to 8 hours, until the chicken is fork-tender and pulls apart easily.

3. Remove the chicken from the slow cooker. With two forks, pull apart the meat into shredded chunks; return to the slow cooker and stir to combine. Cover and leave on the KEEP WARM setting until ready to serve. Serve spooned onto warmed hamburger buns.

Orange Teriyaki Chicken

Teriyaki is a marinade and a glaze at the same time, and it is one of the most popular Asian flavorings for chicken. While it might suffer from overexposure because there are so many teriyaki sauces now on the market, it is delightful when made from scratch. The secret is the soy sauce–rice wine–brown sugar base that permeates the flesh and cooks up as a thin, flavorful glaze. Serve this over steamed rice. ○ *Serves 2*

COOKER: 1½ to 3 quart
SETTING AND COOK TIME: HIGH for 2½ to 3 hours

4 boneless, skinless chicken thighs
¼ cup regular or low-sodium Japanese soy sauce
2 tablespoons mirin (rice wine) or dry sherry
1 tablespoon light or dark brown sugar
1 clove garlic, crushed
Grated zest of 1 small orange or tangerine
One 1-inch piece fresh ginger, peeled and thinly sliced

1. Spray the inside of the crock with nonstick cooking spray. Heat a small skillet over medium-high heat and add the chicken pieces in a single layer, with the smooth side (formerly the skin side) down. Cook for 2 to 3 minutes, to form a nice browned surface; turn the chicken and brown the second side. Transfer the chicken to the slow cooker, smooth side up.

2. Return the skillet to the stove, turn the heat to medium, and add the soy sauce, mirin, brown sugar, and garlic. Stir to heat and dissolve the brown sugar and any browned particles. Immediately pour the mixture over the chicken in the crock and add the zest and ginger slices. Cover and cook on HIGH for 2½ to 3 hours. Serve hot.

Chicken Bouillabaisse

All along the Mediterranean coast of France, succulent varieties of bouillabaisse are made by experienced old cooks and new young cooks alike. So there is a Provence bouillabaisse, a Marseille bouillabaisse, a Cap Cerbère bouillabaisse, even a Parisian version. It is a favorite Friday meal for Catholics who abstain from eating meat on Fridays. It is so popular that French writers have immortalized it in prose. It is said that bouillabaisse is of divine origin, that the Roman goddess of love, Venus, prepared the saffron-tinted stew for her handsome husband, Vulcan, with fish found only in the Mediterranean. Here I give you a California version with poultry in place of the fish, the handiwork of one of my first cooking mentors, food writer Louise Fiszer. It is fabulously delicious and filling. Serve in shallow bowls, ladling the delicious sauce over the chicken and perching the crunchy, garlicky croutons on the side. ● *Serves 2 with leftovers*

COOKER: 3 quart
SETTING AND COOK TIME: HIGH for 4 to 5 hours

¼ cup olive oil
1 medium-size yellow onion, chopped
1 small fennel bulb, chopped
2 cloves garlic, minced
One 8-ounce can tomato sauce
One 28-ounce can whole plum tomatoes, undrained
½ cup chicken broth, canned or homemade (see page 17)
¼ cup dry white wine
Pinch of saffron threads
1 long strip orange zest
6 boneless, skinless chicken thighs, trimmed of fat
Bouquet garni of a few sprigs of parsley, a sprig of oregano, and
   ½ bay leaf, wrapped in a double layer of cheesecloth and
   tied with kitchen twine

PIMIENTO AND GARLIC SPREAD:

3 cloves garlic, peeled and left whole

3 small slices French bread

1 tablespoon pimientos, drained

1 egg yolk or pasteurized egg replacer equivalent

½ teaspoon crumbled dried oregano

½ cup olive oil

A few drops hot sauce, such as Tabasco

Two to four ½-inch-thick slices French bread or ciabatta, sliced on the diagonal

Salt and freshly ground black pepper to taste

Chopped fresh Italian parsley for serving

1. In a medium-size skillet over medium-high heat, warm the olive oil and cook the onion and fennel until soft, 2 minutes. Add the garlic and cook briefly. Pour the contents of the skillet into the slow cooker and add the tomato sauce, plum tomatoes with their juice, broth, wine, saffron, and orange zest to the crock. Break up the tomatoes with the back of a spoon. Nestle the chicken and *bouquet garni* into the sauce. Cover and cook on HIGH for 4 to 5 hours.

2. While the chicken cooks, make the pimiento and garlic spread. Place the garlic in a food processor and pulse to chop. Add the bread and process to grind; you will have about 3 tablespoons. Add all the rest of the ingredients and pulse until smooth and creamy. Transfer to a bowl and refrigerate until ready to serve.

3. Preheat the oven to 400°F. Place the bread slices on a baking sheet and bake until golden brown around the edges, 7 to 9 minutes. Remove and top with the pimiento and garlic spread.

4. Discard the *bouquet garni* from the crock and season the bouillabaisse with salt and pepper. Serve immediately in shallow soup bowls with each portion sprinkled with parsley, and 1 or 2 croutons on the side.

Sticky Chinese Chicken Wings

C hicken wings, once the last part of the chicken one would want to eat, often look like frog's legs to me, with their spare little shank of meat and drumette section. They are sort of an international food, as they take to all sorts of marinades, each one better than the last. Here is an Asian style and one of the most popular flavorings in which to cook chicken wings, next to Southern barbecue sauce. While deep-frying wings is popular, slow cooking them on high heat is really easy and not messy at all. You can make a whole dinner out of these chicken wings. ○ *Serves 2*

COOKER: 3 quart
SETTING AND COOK TIME: HIGH for 1½ to 2 hours

⅓ **cup soy sauce**
¼ **cup dry red wine**
¼ **cup sugar**
1 clove garlic, crushed
1 teaspoon grated fresh ginger
2 pounds chicken wings, bony wing tips cut off and disjointed, or
    1½ pounds chicken drumettes

1. Spray the inside of the crock with nonstick cooking spray. Mix the soy sauce, red wine, sugar, garlic, and ginger in a heatproof bowl. Heat in the microwave briefly to melt the sugar.

2. Place the chicken wings in the slow cooker and pour over the soy-wine marinade; toss with a wooden spoon to coat. Cover and cook on HIGH for 1½ to 2 hours. Stir gently halfway through cooking with a wooden spoon, bringing the wings on the top to the bottom to coat with sauce. Serve hot with lots of napkins.

Jerked Chicken Drumsticks

Drumsticks are as delicious as thighs, and braising tenderizes drumsticks like no other type of cooking, so I like to find a variety of recipes to make with them. I was going a bit crazy trying to get a nice from-scratch jerk paste that would be easy to make and easy to eat. Bottled sauces were too hot. And then I found dry Jamaican jerk seasoning, as easy as can be, on the spice rack. You make your own quick jerk paste in the food processor and use the more delicious dark meat. Serve with beer, fresh flour tortillas with butter, and rice. For a cooling side dish, drizzle chopped avocado with lime juice and sprinkle with chopped fresh cilantro. ○ *Serves 2*

COOKER: 3 quart
SETTING AND COOK TIME: LOW for 6 to 7 hours, or HIGH for 3 to 4 hours

1 jalapeño chile, stemmed, seeded, and cut in half (if you want a zestier taste, add the seeds)
5 green onions, ends trimmed and cut into pieces
2 tablespoons cider vinegar
2 tablespoons brown sugar
1 tablespoon olive oil
1 tablespoon soy sauce
1 tablespoon Myers's rum (optional)
Juice of 1 lime
2 to 3 teaspoons Jamaican jerk seasoning
¾ teaspoon salt
4 to 6 chicken drumsticks
½ medium-size red bell pepper, sliced
½ medium-size green bell pepper, sliced

1. Place the chile, green onions, vinegar, brown sugar, oil, soy sauce, rum (if using), lime juice, jerk seasoning, and salt in a food processor; puree until smooth.

2. Spray the inside of the crock with nonstick cooking spray. Place the drumsticks in the slow cooker, laying them side by side. Pour the seasoning paste over the chicken and turn to coat the pieces, using a small spatula. Add the bell pepper strips. Cover and cook on LOW for 6 to 7 hours (or on HIGH for 3 to 4 hours), until the chicken is cooked through. Serve hot.

Braised Chicken Drumsticks with Garbanzos and Dried Fruit

Tagine stews are usually made in large amounts suitable to serving a family or guests. Here is a nice small tagine, with just enough for two but with all the flavor and lovely earthy ingredients. Moroccan cooking boasts its own warming spice blends, some even including rosebuds or lavender flowers along with allspice berries, fennel seeds, cardamom pods, peppercorns, and sesame seeds. If you have preserved lemons (see page 116) in the fridge, chop some and add them at the end of cooking. Serve with white or whole wheat couscous or an aromatic long-grain rice. ○ *Serves 2*

COOKER: 1½ or 3 quart
SETTINGS AND COOK TIMES: LOW for 6 to 7 hours, or
　　HIGH for 3 to 4 hours; HIGH for last 15 minutes

2 small white boiling onions, sliced

½ medium-size red bell pepper, cut into 1-inch pieces

¾ cup canned garbanzo beans, rinsed and drained

3 tablespoons chopped fresh cilantro

4 dried apricot halves, each cut into quarters

2 tablespoons golden raisins

1 cup chicken broth, canned or homemade (see page 17)

1½ teaspoons cider vinegar

¼ teaspoon paprika

¼ teaspoon ground cinnamon

¼ teaspoon ground cumin

Pinch of ground mace

Pinch of ground ginger

Pinch of cayenne pepper

½ teaspoon salt

2 tablespoons olive oil

4 chicken drumsticks

A few strips of orange zest

1 tablespoon cornstarch

1. Spray the inside of the crock with nonstick cooking spray. Place the onions, bell pepper, garbanzos, cilantro, apricots, and raisins in the slow cooker. Add ¾ cup of the broth, the vinegar, paprika, cinnamon, cumin, mace, ginger, cayenne pepper, and salt.

2. Heat the oil in a small skillet over medium heat and add the chicken legs. Cook until the chicken is browned, about 5 minutes; add to the crock, laying the pieces side by side.

3. Cover and cook on LOW for 6 to 7 hours (or on HIGH for 3 to 4 hours), until the chicken is cooked through. Remove the chicken legs from the crock with a slotted spoon to a plate; cover with foil and keep warm.

4. Increase the heat to HIGH. Whisk together the remaining ¼ cup chicken broth, the orange zest, and the cornstarch in a small bowl; stir into the vegetables and broth in the crock. Return the chicken to the crock, cover, and continue to cook for 15 minutes, until sauce is thickened. Serve hot.

•• Preserved Lemons ••

Preserved lemons are a tart and salty lemon pickle and are one of the characteristic flavors specific to Moroccan cuisine. I love them but don't usually want to make a big batch since I use them sparingly, so here is a nice small batch for other cooks like me. The lemons are boiled gently to jump-start the softening of the rind. "Quick" in this recipe, by the way, means a sped-up 5 to 6 days of brining as opposed to 5 to 6 weeks! You will need to use sterilized canning jars for this recipe; follow the instructions that come with the jars. Use the chopped-up lemons to finish tagine-style stews such as the Braised Chicken Drumsticks with Garbanzos and Dried Fruit (page 114) or Tagine of Lamb, Tomato, Green Beans, and Sesame (page 164), tossed with rice or couscous, or in salads. You might just get hooked.

Quick Preserved Lemons o Makes 2 lemons in a pint jar

2½ cups water
3½ tablespoons kosher salt
2 unblemished, small, organically grown lemons, scrubbed
2 whole cloves
1 teaspoon whole white or black peppercorns
1 cinnamon stick
1 teaspoon whole coriander seed
Freshly squeezed lemon juice as needed

1. In a small saucepan, bring the water to a boil. Add the salt. Cut a thin, dime-size piece from both ends of each lemon. Set a lemon on one end and make vertical cuts ¼ inch deep and 1 inch apart, from top to bottom around the fruit. Repeat with the other lemon. Slip the lemons into the boiling water; reduce the heat to a simmer, cover, and cook until tender when pierced with a knife, about 10 minutes.

2. With a slotted spoon, transfer the lemons to a sterilized wide-mouthed pint glass canning jar. Reserve the salted water. Add the cloves, peppercorns, cinnamon stick, and coriander seeds to the jar. Press down on the lemons to release their juice, and add the salted water to cover the lemons. Seal with the screw-top or spring-top lid and set aside on the kitchen counter to cool completely, then refrigerate. Make sure the lemons are covered with juice at all times, adding a small amount of fresh lemon juice if necessary.

3. The lemons will be ready to use after 5 days, and they will keep in the refrigerator for 3 months. To use, lift out of the liquid, scrape out the soft pulp, and sliver or chop the peels and add to recipes. Rinse them lightly to remove some of the salt, if you wish. You will not use the pickling spices.

M's Turkey Taco Salad

(I) love this salad so much that I want every person who ever reads my books to know how to make it. This recipe is a specialty of my friend M Quento. M uses vine-ripened tomatoes, either salad or Romas, and a thick commercially jarred salsa, like Pace Picante. She likes to use a medium hotness for cooking, but a mild version for serving as a topping. If you're in a hurry, you can cook the meat on HIGH for about 1½ to 2 hours. The slow cooker makes delicious hot taco meat, and it is also good reheated the next day for another salad, poured over a split soft hamburger bun, or spooned into a crisp taco shell. ● *Serves 2 with leftovers*

COOKER: 1½ to 3 quart
SETTING AND COOK TIME: LOW for 4 to 6 hours, or HIGH for 1½ to 2 hours

TACO TURKEY:
1¼ pounds ground dark turkey meat
One 16-ounce jar tomato salsa

FOR THE SALAD:
3 to 4 cups coarsely shredded or chopped iceberg or romaine lettuce
1½ cups corn chips
1 cup canned pinto beans, heated in a saucepan or microwave
¾ cup shredded cheddar cheese
Chunky fresh tomato salsa to taste
1 medium-size ripe tomato, coarsely chopped
½ cup cold sour cream
1 medium-size firm, ripe avocado, pitted, peeled, and sliced right before serving
One 4-ounce can sliced black olives

1. Spray the inside of the crock with nonstick cooking spray. Place the ground turkey and the salsa in the cooker and stir. Cover and cook on LOW for 4 to 6 hours or HIGH for 1½ to 2 hours, until thoroughly cooked. Stir to combine.

2. Assemble all of the salad ingredients in separate containers. To serve, prepare individual plates with layers of lettuce, a handful of corn chips, the hot turkey meat, a spoonful or two of hot pinto beans, shredded cheese, spoonfuls of salsa, diced tomato, sour cream, avocado slices, and olives.

Smoky Chipotle Turkey Breast

Here I use a non-tomato-based barbecue sauce created by Jacquie Hiquera McMahan for her self-published *Chipotle Chile Cookbook* (Olive Press, 1994); it is perfect for the slow cooker and, used as a cooking glaze, makes this turkey breast incredibly special. Serve with roasted seasonal vegetables and a green salad. Or go straight to making hot open-faced sandwiches with melted Monterey Jack cheese and a cranberry sauce (see pages 134–135).

○ *Serves 2 with leftovers*

COOKER: 3 quart, oval preferred
SETTING AND COOK TIME: HIGH for 4 to 5 hours

HONEY-CHIPOTLE GLAZE:
1 clove garlic, peeled and left whole
2 tablespoons chopped fresh cilantro
2 tablespoons chipotle paste (see Note)
2 tablespoons honey
2 tablespoons apple cider vinegar
1 tablespoon brown sugar
1 tablespoon whole-grain Dijon mustard
Pinch of salt
Pinch of ground cumin

1 large yellow onion, sliced
One 2½- to 3-pound bone-in turkey breast half
¼ cup beer of your choice
1 lime, sliced

1. To make the glaze, place the garlic and cilantro in a small food processor; pulse to chop finely. Add the chipotle paste, honey, vinegar, brown sugar, mustard, salt, and cumin; process for 30 seconds to make a smooth puree.

2. Spray the inside of the crock with nonstick cooking spray. Arrange the onion slices in the bottom of the slow cooker. Place the turkey breast, breast side up, on top of the onions; pour in the beer. Spread all of the honey-chipotle glaze over the surface of the turkey. Cover the surface of the breast with the lime slices. Cover and cook on HIGH for 4 to 5 hours. Don't peek. The turkey is done when the internal temperature reaches 170° to 180°F on an instant-read thermometer.

3. When the turkey is cooked, remove with tongs from the crock and place on a platter; cover with foil and let stand for 10 minutes before carving. There will be plenty of liquid from the turkey. Strain the cooking liquid through a cheesecloth-lined colander and press to squeeze the juice from the onions. Place the liquid in a small saucepan. Heat to boiling and reduce a bit. Serve the turkey sliced with the juice on the side.

Note: Since I don't like to fuss with rehydrating dried chiles or opening a new can of them every time I want some chipotles, I puree the contents of a can of chipotles in adobo sauce in the food processor, a tip à la Jacquie the chile queen. I then scrape the mixture into an airtight glass jar and keep it in the refrigerator. It is a snap to stir into a glaze, as above, or into mayonnaise, a pot of chili, sauces, or soups. This keeps for several months and is an incredible convenience.

An alternate method for preserving an opened can of chipotles is to freeze the chiles individually on a parchment paper–lined plate. When frozen, place them in a small freezer bag, and you will be able to remove individual chiles when you need them.

Holiday Turkey Breast with Cranberry-Sage Stuffing

This is the version of slow-cooked turkey breast to make when you have two for a winter holiday dinner, although I enjoy it just as much in the summer. The breast is baked right on top of the layer of savory, moist stuffing. While a turkey breast half is more than adequate for two people in one sitting, I love the leftovers—either a turkey sandwich the next day, some turkey salad stuffed in a pita with curried mayonnaise, or simply another little meal with gravy and stuffing. The oval cooker is best for this so that the turkey breast fits properly. ○ *Serves 2 with leftovers*

COOKER: 3 quart, oval preferred
SETTING AND COOK TIME: LOW for 7 to 9 hours

One 8-ounce package seasoned stuffing mix
2 medium-size shallots, finely chopped
2 stalks celery with leaves, chopped
¼ cup chopped fresh Italian parsley
2 tablespoons chopped dried cranberries
2 teaspoons chopped fresh sage
½ cup hot water or chicken broth
2½ tablespoons unsalted butter
One 2½- to 3-pound bone-in turkey breast half
Salt and freshly ground black or white pepper to taste

GRAVY:
One 1.2-ounce package turkey gravy mix (I use Knorr brand)
⅞ cup water
⅓ cup Madeira

1. Spray the inside of the slow cooker with nonstick cooking spray. Place the stuffing mix loosely in the bottom of the slow cooker. Add the shallots, celery, parsley, cranberries, and sage; toss to combine evenly. In a small bowl, combine the hot water and butter; stir to melt the butter. Pour over the stuffing to moisten evenly; add more liquid if you want a moister stuffing.

2. Place the turkey breast, breast side up, on the bed of stuffing; you can nestle it down a bit. I usually take out one-third of the stuffing, put in the turkey, and put the stuffing back around the sides. Sprinkle the turkey with salt and pepper. Cover and cook on LOW for 7 to 9 hours. Don't lift the lid until 6 hours to test. The turkey is done when the internal temperature reaches 170° to 180°F on an instant-read thermometer. The breast will not be browned.

3. Remove the breast to a carving board and cover with foil to let stand for a few minutes before slicing. Cover the cooker and let the stuffing set while making the gravy.

4. To make the gravy, combine the gravy mix, water, and Madeira in a small saucepan over medium-high heat. Blend with a whisk, stirring constantly, bringing to a boil. Reduce the heat to a simmer and cook for 2 minutes, until thickened.

5. Serve the sliced hot turkey with the stuffing on the side and the gravy poured over all.

Red Wine Turkey Stew with Buttermilk Biscuit Dumplings

T his is a stew from my mother's files, laden with turkey and vegetables, adapted for the slow cooker. She created this when turkey parts were just starting to be common in the supermarket and it was still considered a travesty to have turkey other than at Christmas or Thanksgiving. In my family, though, we were thrilled to see turkey in May, since we all loved it. The stew uses red wine with the turkey tenderloin instead of the more predictable white wine, to a delicious end. You can opt to pass on the dumplings, if you wish, but they are delicious. ○ *Serves 2*

COOKER: 3 quart

SETTINGS AND COOK TIMES: LOW for 2 to 2½ hours, then HIGH for 25 to 35 minutes; dumplings added during last 25 to 35 minutes

½ to ¾ pound turkey tenderloin, cut into large chunks

Salt and freshly ground black pepper to taste

2 tablespoons olive oil

½ cup chopped onion

1 clove garlic, minced

1 medium-size carrot, thinly sliced

1 medium-size parsnip, thinly sliced

2 to 4 small red potatoes, quartered

1 tablespoon all-purpose flour

½ teaspoon chopped fresh thyme leaves

1 cup chicken or vegetable broth, canned or homemade (see page 17 or 18)

¾ cup dry red wine

¼ cup chopped fresh Italian parsley

4 ounces white or cremini mushrooms, quartered

1 recipe dough from Slow Cooker Buttermilk Biscuit Dumplings (page 226)

1. Spray the inside of the crock with nonstick cooking spray. Sprinkle the turkey pieces with salt and pepper. In a large heavy skillet, heat the olive oil and brown the turkey on all sides for a few minutes only. Transfer with tongs to the slow cooker.

2. Add the onion, garlic, carrot, parsnip, and potatoes to the hot skillet with another tablespoon of oil, if necessary (often I will brown the potatoes separately). Sauté until just beginning to soften, 5 to 8 minutes. Sprinkle with the flour and stir; add to the crock and toss with the meat.

3. Heat the thyme, broth, and wine in a measuring cup in the microwave until boiling; add to the crock. Place the parsley and mushrooms on top. Cover and cook on LOW for 2 to 2½ hours, until the meat shows no pink and the vegetables are tender.

4. Prepare the dumplings and slide them into the crock, taking care to place the dumplings on top of solids rather than directly into the liquid, so that they steam nicely on top. Cover and cook on HIGH for 25 to 35 minutes, until the dumplings are cooked through. Pierce the dumplings with a toothpick, bamboo skewer, or metal cake tester; it should come out clean. Serve immediately in soup bowls, with 2 or 3 dumplings per portion.

Poached Turkey Tenderloin with Mango-Ginger Salsa

We poach chicken breasts by the dozens for salads and casseroles, even for a sliced chicken sandwich, but how often do we poach a turkey breast? Here is an ultra-simple recipe to show you how, using boneless turkey tenderloins, and the slow cooker is perfect for the job because it gently cooks the breast until it is oh-so-tender and moist. Here it is served in slices with a fruit salsa, but you may also skip the salsa and shred the poached turkey for use in other recipes, or freeze it for later use. One tenderloin will feed two people.

● *Serves 2 with leftovers; makes about 4 cups shredded or chopped turkey meat*

COOKER: 1½ or 3 quart
SETTING AND COOK TIME: HIGH for 2½ to 3 hours

1¼ to 1½ pounds turkey tenderloins, left whole
Salt and freshly ground black pepper to taste
½ cup chopped celery with leaves
4 green onions, cut into 2-inch pieces
⅔ cup dry white wine

MANGO-GINGER SALSA:
1 medium-size mango, peeled, pitted, and diced
1 medium-size tomato, seeded and diced
⅓ cup diced red bell pepper
3 tablespoons minced red onion
1 tablespoon minced fresh mint
2 teaspoons grated fresh ginger
Juice of 1 lime
Salt to taste

1. Spray the inside of the crock with nonstick cooking spray. Arrange the tenderloins in a single layer in the bottom of the crock. Sprinkle with salt and pepper. Add the celery and onions, then the wine and enough hot water just to cover the turkey. Cover and cook on HIGH for 2½ to 3 hours, until the turkey is white throughout when cut with a knife. The internal temperature will be 170°F. Let stand in the hot broth, uncovered, for 15 minutes.

2. To make the salsa, combine the mango, tomato, bell pepper, onion, mint, ginger, lime juice, and salt in a small bowl. Cover and let stand at room temperature for about 1 hour. (The salsa can be prepared several hours in advance and refrigerated, but it should be served at room temperature.)

3. Remove the turkey from the broth to a plate or cutting board and discard the liquid and vegetables. When cool enough to handle, thinly slice across the grain and serve with the fruit salsa.

4. If you wish to use the poached turkey for another recipe, chop or shred and proceed as directed. Or you may cool the turkey completely in its liquid, then transfer to an airtight container and refrigerate in the liquid for up to 2 days. If not using within 2 days, cool and portion the meat into plastic freezer bags and freeze for up to 2 months.

Jesse's Turkey Shiitake Meatloaf

This meatloaf is from Jesse Cool, who as a food professional wears more hats than anyone I know: food writer, cookbook author, restaurant owner and chef, food-service consultant for the veg-friendly gardener growing her own food, cooking teacher, TV food personality, lecturer on sustainable agriculture, proponent of organic wines, caterer, culinary world traveler, and great home cook with her trio of slow cookers in three different sizes. She is definitely the queen of the crock, and I was lucky to have her contribute one of her great meatloaves for this chapter. "I eat most of my meals in one of my restaurants, but it is just as important to have nurturing, homey food available in my home refrigerator," comments Jesse. "This meatloaf is my favorite. Because it is made with turkey and lots of vegetables, the flavor is extraordinary, but it is light and low calorie." Be sure to use the dark meat, which is half thigh and leg meat; it makes a meatloaf that holds together properly. The breast meat alone is too dry and will fall apart. Jesse uses the mushrooms raw, as in this recipe; I often quickly precook the mushrooms and evaporate some of the liquid in a bit of butter in a hot skillet. This is best made in an oval cooker if you want a traditionally shaped loaf. ● *Serves 2 with leftovers*

COOKER: 1½ to 3 quart
SETTING AND COOK TIME: LOW for 6 to 7 hours, or HIGH for 3 to 4 hours

1¼ pounds ground dark turkey meat
2 eggs, beaten
½ large yellow onion
1 medium-size carrot, cut into chunks
⅓ cup ketchup, plus ½ cup for glazing
2 teaspoons Worcestershire sauce
1 tablespoon dried Italian herbs
1½ teaspoons salt
¼ teaspoon freshly ground black or white pepper
⅓ cup fresh bread crumbs
5 ounces shiitake mushrooms, stems trimmed and coarsely chopped
2 tablespoons chopped fresh Italian parsley

1. Place the ground turkey and eggs in a large mixing bowl. In a food processor, chop the onion and carrot; add to the meat. Add ⅓ cup of the ketchup, the Worcestershire sauce, Italian herbs, salt, pepper, and bread crumbs. Using your hands or a large fork, mix gently but thoroughly, being careful not to compact the meat. Divide the meat in half, shaping one piece into a flat oval (or circle, depending on the shape of your slow cooker) about 8 inches long; sprinkle with the mushrooms and parsley. Then place the rest of the meat mixture on top and pinch the sides to seal the mushrooms inside. Use your hands to shape into a nice fat oval or circle.

2. Spray the inside of the crock with nonstick cooking spray. Make an aluminum foil "cradle" that will help you easily remove the meatloaf from the cooker when it is done. Tear a sheet of foil that is about 14 inches long. Fold in half lengthwise, then in half again lengthwise to make a strip about 3 inches wide. Place the foil strip into the crock lengthwise. The edges of the foil strip will come up the sides of the crock. Place the meat mixture into the crock, on top of the strip, reshaping as necessary. You can also place the meatloaf on a tiny foil-wrapped trivet that fits in your crock, if you like your meatloaf cooked out of its juices. Spread the remaining ½ cup ketchup over the top. Cover and cook on LOW for 6 to 7 hours (or on HIGH for 3 to 4 hours), until an instant-read thermometer inserted into the center of the meatloaf reads 160° to 165°F.

3. To serve, lift the meatloaf onto a cutting board or serving platter, using the foil handles; let stand for 15 minutes before slicing. Slide out and discard the foil strip. Slice the meatloaf and serve hot, or refrigerate and serve cold the next day.

Turkey Pot Roast

One of my oldest cooking friends, Nancyjo Riekse, created this recipe, and I was absolutely delighted with the original concept for turkey in an old-fashioned recipe context. "This is for those of you who have stopped eating red meat but still crave that type of comfort food," she writes. This recipe uses a hindquarter, one big, fat, dark-meat thigh section called the shank that is easily available when the turkeys left over from the holidays are cut into portions to sell quickly. If you cannot find the shank, then substitute two regular turkey thighs that equal the same weight. Make sure the piece of meat can fit in your slow cooker. Serve with one of the delectable cranberry sauces on pages 134–135, or canned jellied cranberry sauce. ◦ *Serves 2 with leftovers*

COOKER: 3 quart, oval preferred
SETTING AND COOK TIME: LOW for 7 to 9 hours

1 turkey hindquarter (about 2 pounds) or 2 turkey thighs
Salt and freshly ground black or white pepper to taste
2 tablespoons olive oil
½ cup chopped onion
1 clove garlic, chopped
½ teaspoon minced fresh basil
¼ teaspoon chopped fresh thyme leaves
1 cup chicken or vegetable broth, canned or homemade (see page 17 or 18)
2 medium-size white potatoes, quartered
2 medium-size carrots, peeled and cut into chunks

1. Spray the inside of the crock with nonstick cooking spray. Sprinkle the turkey with salt and pepper; you can flour it as well if you want a thicker sauce. In a large heavy skillet, heat the olive oil and brown the turkey, skin side down, until a deep golden brown on one side, about 5 minutes. Transfer with tongs to the slow cooker.

2. Add the onion, garlic, basil, thyme, and broth. Place the potatoes and carrots around the sides. Cover and cook on LOW for 7 to 9 hours, until the meat and vegetables are tender.

3. Slice the meat and serve hot with the vegetables, with the cooking liquid drizzled over the top.

Turkey Breast Cutlets with Sweet Potatoes

I wanted to combine turkey and sweet potatoes in a new way. My mother gave me a recipe for meatballs and a cranberry brown gravy from Marcus Samuelsson, lauded chef at the restaurant Aquavit in New York City. So there were the prepackaged turkey breast cutlets in the fresh poultry section, just begging to be included into some slow cooker recipe. Well, here is that incredibly easy gravy over turkey cutlets and sweet potatoes. It is excellent and a complete meal.

o *Serves 2*

COOKER: 3 quart
SETTING AND COOK TIME: LOW for 6 to 7 hours

CRANBERRY BROWN GRAVY:
One 1.2-ounce package turkey gravy mix (I use Knorr brand)
½ cup water
⅓ cup dry white wine
¾ cup whole berry cranberry sauce
2 tablespoons heavy cream
¼ cup dried cranberries

2 medium-size sweet potatoes or Garnet yams, peeled and cut into ⅓-inch-thick slices
4 ounces green beans, ends trimmed and cut into 2-inch pieces
1 large shallot, sliced
1 pound turkey breast cutlets

1. In a small saucepan over high heat, combine the gravy mix, water, wine, and cranberry sauce, and bring to a boil. Reduce to a simmer and whisk until thickened and the cranberry sauce has melted. Stir in the cream and dried cranberries. Set aside.

2. Spray the inside of the crock with nonstick cooking spray. Arrange the sweet potato slices in the bottom of the crock. Then add the green beans and the shallot. Roll up each cutlet and place in a layer on top of the vegetables.

3. Pour the warm cranberry gravy over the cutlets and vegetables. Cover and cook on LOW for 6 to 7 hours, until the turkey and the sweet potatoes are tender.

4. Remove the turkey to a platter, surround with the vegetables, and spoon the gravy over all. Serve immediately.

Braised Herbed Turkey Legs in Riesling

Turkey legs take beautifully to the gentle heat of the slow cooker, becoming tender and savory, yet remaining moist and flavorful. Since my grandfather was born in Alsace Lorraine, the area sandwiched between France and Germany, I have a passion for good Riesling wine, either French or Californian. Season this with the classic French blend of *fines herbes,* or use one herb if you like. Even when the herb department is bare, you can always find parsley! Serve this over wild rice, fluffy couscous, or mashed potatoes. ● *Serves 2*

COOKER: 3 quart, oval preferred
SETTING AND COOK TIME: LOW for 5 to 6 hours

1 tablespoon olive oil
1 tablespoon unsalted butter
2 turkey legs (about 1½ pounds), skin removed
⅓ cup chopped shallots
1 stalk celery, sliced
¼ pound white mushrooms, quartered
⅓ cup Alsatian Riesling
⅓ cup chicken broth, canned or homemade (see page 17)
2 tablespoons *fines herbes*
¼ cup heavy cream
1 tablespoon all-purpose flour combined with 2 tablespoons water
1 tablespoon freshly squeezed lemon juice

1. In a large heavy skillet, heat the oil and butter over medium-high heat. Brown the turkey legs, 2 to 3 minutes per side. Remove them with tongs and place them in the slow cooker.

2. To the fat in the skillet, add the shallots and cook, stirring, until soft, 2 minutes. Add to the crock, along with the celery, mushrooms, wine, broth, and 1 tablespoon of the herbs. Cover and cook on LOW for 5 to 6 hours, until the turkey is tender.

3. Remove the turkey from the crock with tongs and cover with foil to keep warm while you finish the sauce. Pour the contents of the crock into a small saucepan over high heat and add the remaining 1 tablespoon of herbs. Bring it to a boil and boil for 4 to 5 minutes to reduce the sauce and concentrate the flavors. Stir in the cream and the flour-water mixture; whisk until thickened, 2 to 3 minutes. Stir in the lemon juice.

4. Serve the turkey, on or off the bone, with the vegetable-herb sauce spooned over the top.

Food Safety

Is a slow cooker safe for cooking food? Yes, emphatically yes. Even though the countertop slow cooker cooks foods slowly at a relatively low temperature—between 200° and 300°F—the food is definitely safe. The low heat does a better job than faster, higher heat methods in helping less expensive, leaner cuts of meat become tender and experience less shrinkage (high heat shrinks protein in meat and leads to more loss of the natural juices). The direct, multidirectional heat from the pot, lengthy cooking, and concentrated steam created within the tightly covered container all combine to destroy bacteria and make the slow cooker safe for cooking foods. Remember, the food reaches 140°F quickly, which is the safe temperature for food. As a criterion for comparison, pork is considered safe to eat at 138°F.

Turkey Thighs Carbonnade

Any time you see a recipe that uses the word "carbonnade," that is a tip-off that it is made in the manner of the Belgian stew that uses plenty of onions and dark beer as the flavorful liquid to tenderize the meat. This recipe for turkey thighs comes from Little Ricky Rodgers, chef extraordinaire, who was named cooking teacher of the year by *Bon Appétit* magazine, and our very own Mr. Turkey 101. Noodles are a must with this. ● *Serves 2 with leftovers*

COOKER: 3 quart
SETTING AND COOK TIME: LOW for 6 to 8 hours

2 turkey thighs (about 2 pounds), skin and excess fat removed
Salt and freshly ground black or white pepper to taste
2 tablespoons olive oil
½ teaspoon dried thyme
1 bay leaf
2 medium-size yellow onions, chopped
2 cloves garlic, chopped
1 cup dark beer
1 cup chicken broth, canned or homemade (see page 17)
2 tablespoons Dijon mustard
2 tablespoons brown sugar
2 tablespoons unsalted butter
2 tablespoons all-purpose flour

1. Spray the inside of the crock with nonstick cooking spray. Sprinkle the turkey thighs with salt and pepper. In a large heavy skillet, heat the olive oil and brown the turkey until a deep golden brown on one side, about 5 minutes. Transfer with tongs to the slow cooker. Sprinkle with the thyme and add the bay leaf.

2. Add the onion to the skillet and cook until golden. Add the garlic and stir to soften. Add the beer, broth, mustard, and brown sugar; bring to a boil, scraping up the browned bits at the bottom of the skillet. Pour over the turkey in the crock. Cover and cook on LOW for 6 to 8 hours, until the meat is tender.

3. Skim any fat off the top, if necessary. In a small saucepan, melt the butter over medium heat. Add the flour and stir until it just begins to brown to make a roux. Add 1 cup of the hot cooking liquid from the crock to the roux, whisking, and cook until thickened, 2 minutes. Pour the mixture back into the crock and stir. Season to taste. Serve hot.

What would a chapter on turkey be without some fabulous cranberry sauces to serve with it? Turkey just tastes better with tart cranberries to counterpoint the sweetness of the meat. Here are some of my favorites. Be sure to use those bags of fresh cranberries within two weeks of purchase so that they won't get mushy or shriveled; any leftover cranberries can be frozen.

I recommend that you make the salsa on the stovetop, but the other two recipes can also be made in the slow cooker. To make the Cranberries Cabernet or Ro's Cranberry-Raspberry Conserve in the slow cooker, combine the cranberries, sugar, and water or wine in the crock, or in the order as written for the stovetop ingredients. Cover and cook on HIGH for about 2 hours; the cranberries will pop open. Stir in the rest of the ingredients as directed in the recipe. Cool in the crock to room temperature with the lid off.

Cranberries Cabernet ● Makes about 1¼ cups

Everyone seems to have a favorite cranberry sauce, and this one is mine. It comes from food maven Peggy Fallon. This goes with the Thanksgiving turkey and other meats and poultry, of course, but it also makes an interesting flavor counterpoint when served alongside turkey meatloaf. It is so versatile that you can even spoon it over vanilla ice cream!

¾ cup sugar
½ cup Cabernet Sauvignon
1 orange or tangerine, preferably seedless, cut in half
2 whole cloves
1½ cups (6 ounces) fresh or frozen cranberries
One 3-inch cinnamon stick

1. Combine the sugar and wine in a deep, medium-size saucepan over medium heat. Bring to a boil, stirring to dissolve the sugar. Cut the orange in half and stud each half with a clove. Squeeze the juice from the orange into the pot; then add the orange halves. Stir in the cranberries and cinnamon stick and bring back to a boil over medium-high heat. Reduce the heat to medium-low and boil gently until the berries just begin to burst, 5 to 10 minutes.

2. Remove the pan from the heat and let cool to room temperature. Discard the orange, cinnamon, and cloves. Transfer to an airtight container and refrigerate until cold and thickened, at least 2 hours. Serve slightly chilled or at room temperature.

Ro's Cranberry-Raspberry Conserve o Makes about 1½ cups

This is the creation of my friend and in-home chef Rosmarie Finger. The cranberries and raspberries are natural complements to each other, and the raspberries are cooked only by the heat of the finished sauce, with the resulting contrast in texture being satisfying with all sorts of roasted meats like poultry, pork loin, and ham, as well as turkey.

3 tablespoons coarsely chopped walnuts
½ cup sugar
½ cup water
1½ cups (6 ounces) fresh or frozen cranberries
1 tablespoon orange liqueur, such as Grand Marnier
Grated zest of 1 small orange
½ pint fresh raspberries

1. Preheat the oven to 325°F. Place the walnuts on a baking sheet and lightly toast for 4 minutes; set aside.

2. In a deep medium-size saucepan, combine the sugar and water over high heat and bring to a boil. Add the cranberries. Return to a boil, then lower the heat and cook until the berries begin to pop open, about 15 minutes.

3. Remove from the heat and stir in the Grand Marnier, orange zest, walnuts, and raspberries. Scrape with a rubber spatula into an airtight container; let stand until cool. Serve chilled.

Cranberry-Orange Salsa o Makes about 1½ cups

Jacquie Hiquera McMahan is a whiz with all things chile, and here is a spicy, fresh salsa that will leave you scraping the bowl and wanting more. Serve it with turkey and chicken.

2 cups (8 ounces) fresh cranberries
¼ of a medium-size red onion
¼ cup fresh orange juice
Juice of 1 small lime
½ of a jalapeño chile, seeded, stemmed, and minced
¼ cup packed light brown sugar
1 tablespoon honey

Place the cranberries and onion in a food processor and coarsely chop. Place in a medium-size saucepan with the rest of the ingredients. Bring to boil over high heat. Reduce to a simmer and cook, uncovered, for about 10 minutes; do not overcook. The salsa should retain its bright color and firm texture. Serve chilled or at room temperature.

Turkey Thighs, Acorn Squash, and Apples

There are never enough wonderful ways to cook the myriad of winter squash that are available. Here is an easy winter one-pot meal that fills the kitchen with a delightful aroma. Calvados is a strong apple brandy that is made in Normandy, France. Serve with couscous, rice, or cornbread. ● *Serves 2*

COOKER: 3 quart
SETTING AND COOK TIME: LOW for 5½ to 6½ hours

1 pound acorn squash, stemmed, seeded, and cut into 1-inch-thick rings
¾ pound large tart cooking apples, such as Granny Smith,
    cored and cut into ½-inch-thick rings
2 turkey thighs (about 2 pounds), skin and excess fat removed
Salt and freshly ground black or white pepper to taste
1 shallot, chopped
¼ cup unfiltered apple juice or sweet cider
1 tablespoon Calvados
3 tablespoons brown sugar
½ teaspoon ground cinnamon
¼ teaspoon ground allspice

1. Spray the inside of the crock with nonstick cooking spray. Layer the squash and apple rings in the bottom. Place the turkey thighs on top and sprinkle with salt, pepper, and the shallot.

2. In a small bowl, combine the apple juice, Calvados, brown sugar, cinnamon, and allspice; pour over the turkey. Cover and cook on LOW for 5½ to 6½ hours, until the meat is tender. Serve immediately.

Global Flavors
Pork and Lamb

continued

After beef, pork is the most popular meat because it is lean and tender. Pork has a delicate, mild flavor that complements many types of sauces and ingredients, and it cooks well in the moist-heat environment of the slow cooker. It likes barbecue sauces, tomato sauces, and cream sauces, and the strong flavors of sauerkraut, salsa, soy sauce, and ginger. It pairs well with fruit like pineapple, rhubarb, and apples as much as it does with stronger vegetables like turnips and peppers of all sorts. It soaks up wines and liquors like whiskey and rum, adding to the layers of flavors.

Since pork today is so lean and contains much less collagen tissue than beef, it is important to get the right cuts that will cook best in the slow cooker. Pork tenderloin roast, pork rib eyes, the shoulder, spareribs, loin and shoulder chops, ham, bacon, and sausage are the very best cuts for the small slow cooker. The hind leg is the ham. Usually too large for two people, there are now petit hams that weigh less than two pounds, cut from the very bottom of the leg; they are perfect for the small slow cooker. The pork shank is also known as the hock, and is usually used cured and as a flavor addition, most commonly in beans. The back or loin section is the least used for slow cooking, but I have found that the strip of pork tenderloin, one of the leanest of all meats, functions beautifully in the slow cooker since the moisture keeps it from drying out; there are a few recipes here that highlight its versatility. It is the perfect-size roast for one or two people. The shoulder is the best cut for stew and ground for meatballs; that bit of white fat makes for tender eating hours later.

When buying pork, look for firm, moist, pale reddish-pink meat with a fine grain (never gray or red). Overcook pork and it tends to shrink up rather than soften, so take care not to overcook it. At the same time, pork is never cooked rare; it will register about 145°F on an instant-read thermometer when cooked to medium and

160°F when well done. Testing with a thermometer is recommended when in doubt.

If you use any type of pork sausages, unless you buy them fully cooked, you must brown and cook them before adding to the slow cooker, or remove the casing and cook the crumbled meat. Parcook or fully cook bacon as directed in recipe instructions for the slow cooker. Never add raw sausage or bacon to the slow cooker.

Sometimes lamb is thought of as a seasonal meat, referring to animals born in the spring, but with the convenience and availability of New Zealand lamb, excellent lamb is available year round. Lamb is delicate and pairs well with the classics of onion, carrot, and celery, and also with eggplant, mushrooms, sausage, paprika, ham, artichokes, potatoes, all manner of spices and herbs, and, of course, mint jelly.

Most year-round lamb is between 6 and 12 months of age at slaughter. Spring lamb is 3 to 6 months of age and is really a specialty; it is very tender and I do not call for it in any of these recipes, although you can use it, if you wish. When purchasing lamb, look for a firm, dark reddish meat with a fine grain and a fresh smell. The fat will be white. If it smells gamey, it has been kept too long before sale.

Lamb is divided into portions: shoulders, forelegs, breast, ribs, and loin. The best portions for slow cooker braising are the shoulder and tough foreleg, known as the shank. The lamb shoulder, either bone in or boneless, is cooked as a whole roast (it is also called the lamb butt) or cut into stew meat. The shoulder chops are a wonderful braising cut as well. They have a piece of the round foreleg bone embedded. They are tough, but become unbelievably tender and delicious when braised. Regular shoulder chops can be substituted, if you wish. If you love lamb stew, try a lamb neck (a favorite of Julia Child); it is really excellent for full-flavored stews, quite similar in consistency and delicate flavor to oxtail. Many cooks combine two cuts of lamb in their stews. Leg of lamb can be cut up for stew, though it is leaner than the shoulder. I recommend that you cut your own stew meat if you are so inclined, or ask the butcher to help you; prepackaged cut-up lamb stew meat is usually miscellaneous leftovers. Lamb shanks are one of the most succulent and exciting meats to prepare in the slow cooker; they end up melting off the bone, rather than getting a bit tough and dry as with regular roasting methods. They take lovingly to the long braise, and you can flavor them in a myriad of ways.

Many people say they do not like lamb because of its strong flavor. This flavor is often caused by fat left on during cooking. There is an outer membrane on most cuts and, when not removed, there is a definite strong aroma that permeates the flavor as well. Remove this papery membrane before cooking. Lamb fat congeals quickly, so you can easily remove the surface fat from a stew right after cooking, or chill it and lift it off before serving.

Braised Pork Chops
with Turnips and Apples

This is an excellent French-style dish combining pork with turnips and apples, especially suited to fall and winter dining pleasure. Serve with French Pilaf (page 213) or boiled potatoes and a green salad with watercress.

○ *Serves 2*

COOKER: 1½ to 3 quart
SETTING AND COOK TIME: LOW for 6 to 7 hours

1 tablespoon olive oil
1 tablespoon unsalted butter
Two 1-inch-thick boneless center-cut pork chops or shoulder chops
Salt and freshly ground black pepper to taste
2 shallots, sliced
1 tart cooking apple, peeled, cored, and sliced into wedges
1 medium-size or 2 small turnips, trimmed, peeled, and
    sliced into wedges the same size as the apples
¼ cup apple juice or apple cider
2 teaspoons Dijon mustard
2 to 3 tablespoons crème fraîche

1. In a heavy skillet over high heat, melt the olive oil and butter together and quickly sear and brown the pork chops on both sides. Place in the slow cooker. Sprinkle with salt and pepper.

2. Quickly sauté the shallot in the pan and place in the slow cooker, along with the apple and turnip. Blend the apple juice with the mustard and pour into the crock. Cover and cook on LOW for 6 to 7 hours, until the meat is tender.

3. Transfer the chops, apples, and turnips to a platter. Turn the cooker to HIGH and whisk in the crème fraîche. Add salt to taste and pour the sauce over the pork. Serve immediately.

Pork Chops with Sauerkraut and New Potatoes

his is one of my favorite dishes. Serve it with whole-berry cranberry sauce, or applesauce and creamed horseradish. I vary the paprika, using either sweet, hot, or smoked. If you want to make this like *szekely goulash,* a Hungarian specialty and a real treat for me when I was growing up, simply remove the pork chops when done, then stir $\frac{1}{3}$ cup sour cream mixed with 2 tablespoons buttermilk into the sauerkraut and potatoes. ○ *Serves 2*

COOKER: 1½ to 3 quart
SETTING AND COOK TIME: LOW for 6 to 7 hours

1 tablespoon olive oil
Two 1-inch-thick boneless center-cut pork chops or shoulder chops
4 red or white new potatoes, thickly sliced
Salt and freshly ground black pepper to taste
Paprika to taste
1 shallot or white boiling onion, minced
One 16-ounce bag or jar fresh sauerkraut, rinsed and drained
1 tablespoon dry white wine or champagne

1. In a heavy skillet over high heat, heat the olive oil and quickly sear and brown the pork chops on both sides.

2. Place the potatoes in the bottom of the slow cooker. Place the pork chops on the bed of potatoes. Sprinkle with salt, pepper, paprika, and the shallot. Arrange the sauerkraut over the pork chops, then sprinkle with the wine. Cover and cook on LOW for 6 to 7 hours, until the meat is tender. Serve immediately.

Mexican Pork Chops

T he picante tomato salsa we are most familiar with is *salsa mexicana* or *pico de gallo,* a raw table sauce or relish eaten as a condiment as opposed to a cooked sauce. Salsas contain some chiles in their ripe juiciness, either smoked or fresh, and a bit of onion or garlic. Use your choice of salsa as a sauce for these pork chops; it will melt into a fresh, bright cooked sauce to serve with rice. A quick squeeze of the three citrus juices makes an equivalent to the Seville bitter orange, a uniquely flavored fruit used as a vinegar substitute in Mexico. ◉ *Serves 2*

COOKER: 1 ½ to 3 quart
SETTING AND COOK TIME: HIGH for 3 to 4 hours

2 teaspoons olive oil
Two 1-inch-thick boneless center-cut pork chops
⅔ cup chunky tomato salsa, fresh or jarred
1 tablespoon freshly squeezed lime juice
1 tablespoon freshly squeezed orange juice
Squeeze of fresh grapefruit juice

1. In a heavy skillet over high heat, heat the olive oil and quickly sear and brown the pork chops on both sides. Place the pork chops in the slow cooker.

2. In a small bowl, combine the salsa and juices, and pour over the pork. Cover and cook on HIGH for 3 to 4 hours, until the meat is tender. Serve immediately.

Pork Stew Peperonata

T he assertiveness of bell peppers makes a perfect foil for sweet pork. Sometimes you can find canned yellow tomatoes; if so, grab a few cans to make this thick stew. It is adapted from a recipe by another of my favorite food writers and chefs, Rick O'Connell of San Francisco. This is even better when made a day ahead, and is good piled into pita halves to make sandwiches. ○ *Serves 2*

COOKER: 3 quart
SETTING AND COOK TIME: HIGH for 3 to 3½ hours, or LOW for 5 to 6 hours;
 fresh herbs added during last 15 to 30 minutes

1¼ to 1½ pounds boneless pork loin, cut into 1-inch pieces
½ teaspoon salt
¼ teaspoon freshly ground black pepper
1 tablespoon olive oil
1 medium-size yellow onion, chopped
2 bell peppers, red and yellow if possible, stemmed, seeded, and cut into 1½-inch squares
½ of a 14.5-ounce can Italian peeled tomatoes or yellow tomatoes, drained and chopped
1 tablespoon chopped fresh Italian parsley
1 tablespoon chopped fresh basil

1. Season the pork with the salt and pepper. In a large skillet over medium-high heat, heat the oil until very hot. Add the pork and cook until browned on all sides, 3 minutes. Transfer to the slow cooker. Add the onion, bell peppers, and tomatoes to the crock. Cover and cook on HIGH for 3 to 3½ hours (or on LOW for 5 to 6 hours).

2. Carefully remove the lid and stir in the parsley and basil. Cover and cook another 15 to 30 minutes, until the pork is tender enough to cut with a fork. Season to taste and serve hot.

Lions' Heads

Don't pass this recipe by because you think it is too exotic or difficult. Simply pork meatballs with cabbage, this is one of the famous homey dishes in Chinese cuisine, traditionally simmered in a clay braising pot. Upon serving, each meatball symbolically resembles the head of a lion with a mane of cabbage leaves, a nod to China's legacy of metaphorical recipe names commanding the diner's attention during elaborate banquets. This should be made with ground pork shoulder, since some fat is necessary to keep the meatballs together properly. Be sure to use fresh ground pork the same day you buy it; it is a delicate meat that sours quickly. ● *Serves 2*

COOKER: 3 quart
SETTING AND COOK TIME: HIGH for 3 to 4 hours

1½ pounds coarsely ground pork shoulder
1 tablespoon finely minced fresh ginger
1 clove garlic, finely minced
1 egg
2 tablespoons low-sodium soy sauce (or dark soy sauce)
2 tablespoons rice wine or dry sherry
4 teaspoons cornstarch
½ teaspoon salt
1 teaspoon sesame oil
2 to 3 tablespoons peanut oil
1½ pounds napa cabbage
½ cup chicken broth, canned or homemade (see page 17)
Freshly ground white pepper to taste
1½ teaspoons cornstarch dissolved in 2 tablespoons cold water (optional)

1. In a bowl, combine the ground pork, ginger, garlic, egg, 1 tablespoon of the soy sauce, 1 tablespoon of the rice wine, the cornstarch, salt, and sesame oil. Blend thoroughly with your hands, cover with plastic wrap, and let stand for 20 minutes.

2. Form the seasoned pork into 6 large meatballs. In a large skillet, heat the peanut oil and brown the meatballs, using a metal spatula to roll them around carefully.

3. Spray the inside of the crock with nonstick cooking spray and line with several layers of whole outer leaves of the cabbage; use 6 to 8 leaves. Set aside 6 more whole leaves for covering the casserole, and shred the remaining inner leaves; you will have about 4 cups. Transfer the meatballs to the slow cooker. Scatter the shredded cabbage over the meatballs and add the broth, along with the remaining 1 tablespoon soy sauce and 1 tablespoon rice wine. Sprinkle with white pepper. Lay the whole cabbage leaves over the top. Cover and cook on HIGH for 3 to 4 hours, until the meatballs are firm to the touch; an instant-read thermometer inserted into the center of a meatball will read 165°F.

4. Remove and discard the top layer of cabbage. Serve immediately, using a slotted spoon to remove the meatballs and tongs for the shredded cabbage. If you want to thicken the sauce, stir the cornstarch dissolved in water into the liquid in the crock after all the meatballs and shredded cabbage have been removed. Stir until clear and thickened, then pour the sauce over the meatballs.

Tomatillo Pork and Mushrooms

T his was originally a recipe from *Sunset* magazine contributed by a home cook specifically for weekday meals. I went nuts with the convenience of using the two store-bought green Mexican sauces and loved the combination with mushrooms, not often included in Latin recipes. I adapted it for the slow cooker and it took on a new life. Serve with quinoa or rice and corn tortillas. ● *Serves 2*

COOKER: 3 quart
SETTING AND COOK TIME: HIGH for 3 to 3 ½ hours, or LOW for 5 to 6 hours

1¼ to 1½ pounds boneless pork loin or shoulder, cut into 1-inch pieces
½ teaspoon salt
¼ teaspoon freshly ground black pepper
1 tablespoon olive oil
1 medium-size yellow onion, chopped
¾ pound white mushrooms, thickly sliced
1 clove garlic, minced
One 28-ounce can green enchilada sauce
One 7-ounce jar salsa verde (tomatillo salsa)
¼ cup chopped fresh cilantro

1. Season the pork with the salt and pepper. In a large skillet over medium-high heat, heat the oil until very hot. Add the pork and cook until browned on all sides, 3 minutes. Transfer to the slow cooker. Add the onion, mushrooms, garlic, and the two sauces to the crock. Cover and cook on HIGH for 3 to 3½ hours (or on LOW for 5 to 6 hours), until the pork is tender enough to cut with a fork.

2. Stir in the cilantro. Serve hot.

Pork and Celery Stew

Both the Greeks and the Italians mix pork and celery, one of my favorite vegetables. This recipe features a lot of celery in all its glory, instead of just as an aromatic undertone. There will be an almost equal amount of celery and meat in this dish. Serve this with fresh country bread. ❍ *Serves 2*

COOKER: 3 quart

SETTING AND COOK TIME: HIGH for 3 to 3 ½ hours, or LOW for 5 to 6 hours; capers and parsley added halfway through the cooking time

1¼ to 1½ pounds boneless pork shoulder, cut into 1-inch pieces

½ teaspoon salt

¼ teaspoon freshly ground black pepper

1 tablespoon olive oil

3 to 4 large shallots, chopped

6 stalks celery, trimmed and cut into 1½-inch pieces

¼ cup chopped celery leaves

½ cup water

¼ cup dry white wine, such as Soave or Chenin Blanc

½ teaspoon dry mustard, such as Colman's

1 tablespoon capers, drained

2 tablespoons chopped fresh Italian parsley

1. Season the pork with the salt and pepper. In a large skillet over medium-high heat, heat the oil until very hot. Add the pork and cook until browned on all sides, 3 minutes. Transfer to the slow cooker. Add the shallots, celery, celery leaves, water, wine, and mustard to the crock. Cover and cook on HIGH for 3 to 3½ hours (or on LOW for 5 to 6 hours). Halfway through the cooking time, carefully remove the lid and stir in the capers and parsley.

2. Cover and continue to cook until the pork is tender enough to cut with a fork. Season to taste and serve hot.

Jerked Pulled Pork
with Rum Barbecue Sauce

his is one delicious way to braise pork. Pork roast with barbecue sauce is a favorite with all cooks who use the slow cooker, and I keep it really easy with jarred barbecue sauce. Instead of pork shoulder, here it is made with low-fat tenderloin, which is amazing in the slow cooker despite how lean it is. When cooked, shred the meat and pile it onto fresh rolls with more barbecue sauce on top, or use it to top rice. ○ *Serves 2*

COOKER: 1½ to 3 quart
SETTING AND COOK TIME: LOW for 6 to 7 hours

½ teaspoon chili powder or smoked paprika
Pinch of garlic powder
Pinch of ground allspice
Pinch of salt and freshly ground black pepper
1¼ pounds pork tenderloin
Juice of ½ lemon or lime
1 medium-size yellow onion, sliced
1 cup barbecue sauce of your choice
2 tablespoons dark rum

1. Combine the chili powder, garlic powder, allspice, salt, and pepper in a small bowl. Drizzle the tenderloin with the lemon juice, then rub the spices into it. Place the roast in a zipper-top plastic bag and marinate in the refrigerator for 1 to 3 hours, or overnight.

2. Place the onion in the bottom of the slow cooker. Remove the roast from the bag and cut into 1-inch cubes; place on top of the onions. Combine the barbecue sauce and rum in a small bowl; mix well and pour over the roast. Cover and cook on LOW for 6 to 7 hours, until the meat is fork-tender. Pull into shreds with two forks and serve hot.

Pork Tenderloin with Rhubarb

Rhubarb has a short season, and I am always looking for ways to use the pretty, rosy stem other than in pies and cobblers. Here it is part of a delectable Midwest-style savory sauce that goes perfectly with the pork. Remember never to use rhubarb leaves, as they contain oxalic acid, which is poisonous. Dessert wine or even leftover champagne work nicely instead of the dry white wine (each adding a bit different flavor, of course). ○ *Serves 2*

COOKER: 1½ to 3 quart
SETTING AND COOK TIME: LOW for 6 to 7 hours

1¼ pounds boneless pork tenderloin
½ teaspoon ground ginger
1 teaspoon salt
¼ teaspoon coarsely ground black or white pepper
1 tablespoon olive oil
1½ cups diced rhubarb
1 large shallot, chopped
3 tablespoons brown sugar
Pinch of ground cinnamon
Pinch of crumbled dried rosemary
⅓ cup dry white wine
Grated zest of ½ orange

1. Pat the meat dry with paper towels and rub with the ginger, salt, and pepper. In a large skillet over medium-high heat, warm the oil until very hot. Add the meat and cook until browned on all sides, 3 to 4 minutes. Transfer to the slow cooker and arrange it on the bottom.

2. Add the rhubarb and shallot to the pan, cooking for a few minutes, then sprinkle with the brown sugar, cinnamon, and rosemary. Pour the mixture over the tenderloin in the crock. Add the wine, zest, and more pepper to the crock. Cover and cook on LOW for 6 to 7 hours, until the pork is fork-tender.

3. Transfer the pork to a serving platter and let rest for 10 minutes. If you want a thicker sauce, pour the sauce into a saucepan and bring to a boil over high heat, letting it boil until thickened, only a few minutes. Slice the meat into ½-inch-thick portions and spoon the sauce over the top.

Pork Tenderloin with Ginger-Plum Glaze

Asian flavors go naturally with pork, their tangy edge cutting the sweetness of the meat. This recipe features a thick, flavorful glaze based on store-bought plum sauce (also called duck sauce). While this type of high-sugar glaze would burn on a barbecue, it is not a problem in the slow cooker, and the meat can cook in the marinade. You can skip the marinating time, if you like. Serve this with steamed green beans or broccoli. Leftovers are good in fried rice or cut into strips in a salad. ○ *Serves 2*

COOKER: 1½ to 3 quart
SETTING AND COOK TIME: LOW for 6 to 7 hours

1¼ pounds boneless pork tenderloin
⅓ cup store-bought plum sauce
2 tablespoons low-sodium soy sauce
2 tablespoons hoisin sauce
1½ tablespoons dry sherry
1 tablespoon plus 1 teaspoon grated fresh ginger
1 clove garlic, crushed
2 green onions (white and green parts), sliced, for serving

1. Place the tenderloin in a zipper-top plastic bag. Combine the plum sauce, soy sauce, hoisin sauce, sherry, ginger, and garlic in a small bowl; stir until smooth. Pour over the meat, seal, and refrigerate for 4 hours or overnight.

2. Spray the inside of the slow cooker with nonstick cooking spray. Transfer the meat and marinade to the slow cooker and arrange the strip of pork in the bottom. Cover and cook on LOW for 6 to 7 hours, until the pork is fork-tender.

3. Transfer the pork to a serving platter and let rest for 10 minutes. Slice the meat into ½-inch-thick portions and sprinkle with the green onions. Serve hot.

Oscar's Pork Chile Verde

Braised and shredded pork is one of Mexico's mainstay dishes, and there are many variations, since this is true home cooking; it is used for burritos, tacos, and in soups. Here is a chile verde that is simplicity and authenticity itself, from my friend the brilliant Russian-Mexican chef Oscar Mariscal. Bring out the warm flour tortillas and pile the pork filling on top, layered with rice, toasted pine nuts, avocado slices, and cilantro (in that order, and no cheese, please). Fold over and devour. Or serve this as a stew over rice with some cooked small white beans added in, and topped with toasted pine nuts and lots of chopped cilantro.

● *Serves 2*

COOKER: 3 quart
SETTING AND COOK TIME: LOW for 7 to 9 hours

1 large yellow onion, diced
1 yellow bell pepper, stemmed, seeded, and chopped
2 whole fresh jalapeño chiles
1¾ to 2 pounds pork rib eyes (2 to 3 steaks)
Pinch of ground cumin
Pinch of dried oregano
2 sprigs fresh cilantro
½ teaspoon salt, or to taste
Freshly ground black pepper to taste

1. Spray the inside of the crock with nonstick cooking spray and layer the onion, pepper, and chiles in the bottom. Top with the rib eyes. Sprinkle with the cumin and oregano, add the cilantro sprigs, and add water just to cover. Cover and cook on LOW for 7 to 9 hours, until the pork shreds easily when pressed with a spoon.

2. Remove the rib eyes and shred the meat roughly off the bone; discard the bones. Return the meat to the crock with the vegetables. Stir to combine, season with salt and pepper, and serve hot.

Chipotle-Honey Pork Tenderloin with Watermelon Salsa

Here is a terrific flavor combination for pork of any type: smoky chipotle in adobo sauce with honey and lime. The cooling watermelon salsa adds a sweet counterpoint. I keep the extra canned chiles wrapped individually in the freezer so that I can use one or two at a time and not waste the can. This is really toothsome and addictive. ❍ *Serves 2*

COOKER: 1½ to 3 quart
SETTING AND COOK TIME: LOW for 6 to 7 hours

1¼ pounds boneless pork tenderloin
2 to 3 teaspoons chili powder
1 teaspoon salt
⅓ cup honey
3 tablespoons freshly squeezed lime juice
1 chipotle chile in adobo sauce, minced, or 1 tablespoon chipotle paste (see page 119)
1½ tablespoons adobo sauce

WATERMELON SALSA:
2 plum tomatoes, seeded and coarsely chopped
1 cup chopped watermelon
½ cup chopped fresh cilantro
¼ cup diced red onion
¼ cup chopped fresh Italian parsley
1 small jalapeño chile, seeded and finely chopped
2 tablespoons champagne vinegar
2 tablespoons olive oil
Salt to taste

1. Spray the inside of the crock with nonstick cooking spray. Rub the tenderloin with the chili powder and salt. Place the meat into the slow cooker and arrange the strip on the bottom.

2. Place the honey and lime juice in a measuring cup and microwave to melt the honey; stir in the chipotle chile and adobo sauce. Pour the sauce over the meat. Cover and cook on LOW for 6 to 7 hours, until the pork is fork-tender.

3. Make the watermelon salsa by combining all the ingredients in a small bowl, then cover and refrigerate.

4. Transfer the pork to a serving platter and let rest for 10 minutes. Slice the meat into ½-inch-thick portions and serve with the salsa on the side.

·· Slow Cooker Tip ··
Slow Cooker Settings and Temperatures

There are two cook settings on a slow cooker: LOW and HIGH. The LOW setting uses 80 to 185 watts and cooks in the temperature range of 170° to 200°F. The HIGH setting is double the wattage, 160 to 370 watts, and cooks at a temperature of 280° to 300°F, with slight variations due to the size of the cooker, the temperature of the food, and how full the crock is. There is a KEEP WARM setting, but that is not for cooking or reheating food.

Every machine seems to cook a little bit differently, and only by using your machine will you learn how to gauge the time relative to how the food is cooking. To check the temperature of your slow cooker, fill it three-quarters full with water, cover with the lid, and heat on LOW for 8 hours. Lift the lid and check the water temperature with an instant-read dial or digital thermometer. The temperature should read 185°F. If it is a bit higher, you will know to adjust your cooking time slightly down, to prevent overcooking. If the temperature is lower, you may not be reaching the safe temperature of 140°F fast enough and should not use that cooker; exchange or discard it and buy a new one.

Glazed Whole Baby Ham with Pineapple

Rummaging through the pile of hams at my local market, I came across whole baby hams with the bone in. In the same pile were boneless hams, suitable for cooking for two since they were less than 2 pounds. I was delighted. Ham is a delicious meal, but when cooking for one or two, a 5-pound ham is just not practical. No matter what size, make sure the ham you choose will fit into your slow cooker. The glaze makes a very delicious little sauce, and the aroma of the cooking ham is a delight. Use any leftover ham in split pea soup or, of course, in ham sandwiches. ● *Serves 2 with leftovers*

COOKER: 3 quart
SETTING AND COOK TIME: LOW for 5 to 6 hours

One 1½- to 2-pound bone-in or boneless whole ham

BROWN SUGAR MUSTARD GLAZE:
¼ cup packed light or dark brown sugar
1 tablespoon honey
1 tablespoon Dijon mustard
½ cup crushed pineapple with ¼ cup pineapple juice

1. Spray the inside of the crock with nonstick cooking spray. Place the ham in the slow cooker.

2. To make the glaze, combine the brown sugar, honey, and mustard in a small bowl. Spread over the ham with a metal spatula. Pour over the pineapple with its juice. Cover and cook on LOW for 5 to 6 hours, until an instant-read thermometer inserted into the ham reads at least 160°F.

3. Transfer the ham to a platter and pour the sauce into a small gravy boat for serving. Slice the ham and serve hot with some of the sauce spooned over.

Honey Barbecue Pork Ribs

he glaze here is ridiculously simple and splendidly delicious. For extra flavor, coat the ribs with the honey and marinate them overnight in the refrigerator. ○ *Serves 2*

COOKER: 3 quart
SETTING AND COOK TIME: LOW for 7 to 9 hours

2 pounds pork loin back ribs, baby back ribs, or country-style pork spareribs, cut into serving pieces of 3 to 4 ribs
1 small yellow onion, sliced
1 cup store-bought or homemade barbecue sauce of your choice
⅓ cup mild-flavored honey
A few splashes Sriracha hot sauce, or other favorite hot sauce

1. Arrange the rib portions in the slow cooker, layering them with the onion slices.

2. Combine the barbecue sauce, honey, and hot sauce in a small bowl until smooth; spoon over the ribs. If you have a round cooker, stack the ribs with sauce in between. Cover and cook on LOW for 7 to 9 hours, until the meat is tender and starts to separate from the bone.

3. Serve immediately. If there is extra sauce on the bottom of the cooker, transfer to a bowl and serve on the side.

Country Pork Ribs
with Sauerkraut and Pears

S auerkraut has a puckery, sour tang that complements the sweetness of pork perfectly. The accompanying flavors of vermouth, brown sugar, and fruit take the sharp edge off the sauerkraut. Serve this with mashed or boiled potatoes with parsley. ● *Serves 2*

COOKER: 3 quart
SETTING AND COOK TIME: LOW for 7 to 9 hours

1 medium-size yellow onion, sliced ¼ inch thick
1 large, firm pear, peeled, cored, and sliced ½ inch thick
2 pounds bone-in country-style pork spareribs, cut into serving pieces of 3 to 4 ribs
Salt and freshly ground black pepper to taste
One 16-ounce bag or jar fresh sauerkraut, rinsed and drained
2 tablespoons brown sugar
¼ teaspoon whole caraway seeds
¼ cup white vermouth

Layer the onion, pear, and ribs in the slow cooker. Sprinkle with salt and pepper. Arrange the sauerkraut over the ribs, then sprinkle with the brown sugar and caraway seeds. Pour in the vermouth. Cover and cook on LOW for 7 to 9 hours, until the meat is tender and starts to separate from the bone. Serve immediately.

Red Ribs

This Asian glaze is excellent, and the ribs are great for summer buffets with coleslaw, baked beans, and corn on the cob. This glaze is also good on pork tenderloin. ○ *Serves 2*

COOKER: 3 quart
SETTING AND COOK TIME: LOW for 7 to 9 hours

2 pounds pork loin back ribs or country-style pork spareribs,
    cut into serving pieces of 3 to 4 ribs
¼ cup ketchup
2 tablespoons soy sauce
2 tablespoons freshly squeezed lemon juice
2 tablespoons honey
1 tablespoon brown sugar
1 clove garlic, crushed
1 tablespoon grated fresh ginger

Arrange the rib portions in the slow cooker. Combine the ketchup, soy sauce, lemon juice, honey, brown sugar, garlic, and ginger in a small bowl and mix until smooth; spoon over the ribs. If you have a round cooker, stack the ribs with sauce in between. Cover and cook on LOW for 7 to 9 hours, until the meat is tender and starts to separate from the bone. Serve immediately.

Lamb Stew with Lemon and Garlic

This recipe for a traditional Italian lamb stew from Sicily, *stufato d'agnello alla campidanesi,* was contributed by chef and cookbook author Joyce Goldstein. It appears in her book *Enoteca: Simple Delicious Recipes in the Italian Wine Bar Tradition* (Chronicle Books, 2004), and is adapted here for the small slow cooker. It is gloriously simple and nourishing. Joyce serves the stew with roasted red potatoes, but penne pasta is good too. ● *Serves 2*

COOKER: 1½ to 3 quart
SETTING AND COOK TIME: LOW for 6 to 8 hours

3 to 4 tablespoons olive oil
1½ pounds lamb shoulder, trimmed of excess fat and cut into 2-inch pieces
2 medium-size yellow onions, thickly sliced
2 cloves garlic, minced
¼ cup dry white wine
½ cup beef broth, or as needed
3 tablespoons freshly squeezed lemon juice, or more to your taste
Salt and freshly ground black or white pepper to taste

1. Warm 2 tablespoons of the olive oil in a large sauté pan over medium-high heat. Add the lamb, in batches if necessary, and brown quickly on all sides, about 5 minutes. Using a slotted spoon, transfer to the slow cooker.

2. Add the remaining 1 to 2 tablespoons olive oil to the pan and add the onions; sauté briefly until they begin to soften. Add the garlic and sauté for a minute or two, then add the onions and garlic to the lamb in the crock. Add the wine and enough stock just to cover the meat. Cover and cook on LOW for 6 to 8 hours, until the meat is fork-tender.

3. At the end of the cooking time, stir in the lemon juice and season with salt and pepper. Serve hot.

Navarin with Mint and Peas

avarin printanier, as this dish is also known, is a famous French spring lamb and vegetable ragoût. Mint works in the same way as lemon with lamb: it freshens and balances the meat flavors. If you can find fresh shelled English peas, available for a short time in the spring, use them; otherwise frozen will suffice. Serve with egg noodles. ● *Serves 2*

COOKER: 1½ to 3 quart
SETTINGS AND COOK TIMES: LOW for 6 to 8 hours, then HIGH for 20 to 30 minutes; peas added during the last 20 to 30 minutes

1 tablespoon olive oil
2 tablespoons unsalted butter
1½ pounds lamb shoulder or leg of lamb, trimmed of excess fat and cut into 1-inch cubes
2 medium-size shallots, finely chopped
8 baby carrots, each cut into 3 pieces
3 to 4 sprigs fresh mint
½ cup dry white wine
⅓ cup chicken broth, canned or homemade (see page 17)
Salt and freshly ground black or white pepper to taste
1 to 1½ cups shelled fresh peas or thawed frozen garden peas

1. Warm the olive oil and 1 tablespoon of the butter in a large sauté pan over medium-high heat. Add the lamb, in batches if necessary, and brown quickly on all sides, about 5 minutes. Using a slotted spoon, transfer to the slow cooker. Add the shallots, carrots, mint sprigs, wine, and broth to the lamb in the slow cooker. Cover and cook on LOW for 6 to 8 hours, until the meat is fork-tender.

2. At the end of the cooking time, transfer the lamb to a bowl with a slotted spoon, cover, and keep warm. Discard the mint and transfer the carrots to a bowl (I like to eat the carrots separately). Season the sauce with salt and pepper. Turn the heat to HIGH, add the peas, and cover. Cook until the peas are tender, 20 to 30 minutes.

3. Swirl the remaining 1 tablespoon butter into the sauce and return the lamb to the crock. Serve hot.

Lamb Korma

From the country shaped like a diamond, whose inhabitants eat the least amount of meat of any place on the globe, comes this lamb curry with yogurt. Lamb and goat are the main meats of India, reflecting the Persian and Moghul influences in their contemporary cuisine. This recipe came from the original 1970s Conran British cookbook, which states, "This rich, mild, and very delicious curry was a firm favorite with the Madras Club in the nineteenth century," which certainly conjures up visions of the Victorian Raj at its peak. It uses the classic technique of cooking the spices in hot butter to release their essences and then cooking the meat in yogurt, which makes its own sauce with the meat juices. It is finished with lemon juice and toasted cashews. Serve with plain basmati rice and a cucumber salad. ● *Serves 2*

COOKER: 3 quart
SETTING AND COOK TIME: LOW for 6 to 8 hours

1½ teaspoons coriander seeds
1½ pounds lamb stew meat or lamb shoulder,
    trimmed of excess fat and cut into 2-inch pieces
One 1½-inch-thick piece fresh ginger, slivered
Salt and freshly ground black or white pepper to taste
1½ tablespoons unsalted butter
1 clove garlic, chopped
1 large yellow onion, chopped
5 whole green cardamom pods
¼ teaspoon ground cloves
½ teaspoon ground turmeric
⅛ teaspoon ground coriander
½ cup plain whole-milk yogurt
Juice of ½ lemon
3 to 4 tablespoons roasted cashew nuts, coarsely chopped

1. Crush the coriander seeds in a mortar and pestle to a fine powder; set aside.

2. In a large bowl, mix the lamb and slivered ginger and season with salt and pepper. Warm the butter in a large sauté pan over medium-high heat. Add the lamb, in batches if necessary, and brown quickly on all sides, about 5 minutes. Using a slotted spoon, transfer to the slow cooker.

3. Add the garlic and onion to the pan and sauté until softened. Add the cardamom, cloves, turmeric, and coriander and a few grinds of black pepper, stirring for 30 seconds or so. Stir in the yogurt, and then add the mixture to the crock, mixing well with the lamb and ginger. Cover and cook on LOW for 6 to 8 hours, until the lamb is fork-tender.

4. Stir in the lemon juice and the cashews. Cover and let stand for 15 minutes. Serve hot.

Lamb Stew with Peanut Sauce

There is a little-known cookbook that I love, titled *The Supermarket Epicure,* by Joanna Preuss (William Morrow, 1988). I first read some of Joanna's recipes in a newspaper clipping from New Jersey sent by my aunt. Her recipes struck me as fresh and exciting. She has stayed sort of in the background of the food world, teaching cooking locally on the East Coast and building a following. I was delighted to find a copy of her book at my secondhand bookstore. Even though they were written 20 years ago, the recipes are as interesting and delicious as anything created today. Here is her lamb stew with a simple, not too heavy peanut sauce, adapted for the slow cooker. As my slow cooker foodie friend Lynn Alley says, "People love anything with peanut sauce on it, it's so good!" Serve this over brown jasmine rice. ● *Serves 2*

COOKER: 1½ to 3 quart
SETTING AND COOK TIME: LOW for 6 to 8 hours

2 tablespoons olive oil
1½ pounds lamb shoulder, trimmed of excess fat and cut into 1½-inch pieces
1 clove garlic, minced
¼ cup smooth peanut butter
3 tablespoons low-sodium soy sauce
3 tablespoons dark brown sugar
2 tablespoons freshly squeezed lemon juice
1 tablespoon molasses
⅛ teaspoon cayenne pepper
½ cup water
¼ cup chopped roasted peanuts
2 tablespoons chopped fresh cilantro for garnish
Salt and freshly ground black or white pepper to taste

1. Warm the olive oil in a large sauté pan over medium-high heat. Add the lamb, in batches if necessary, and brown quickly on all sides, about 5 minutes. Using a slotted spoon, transfer to the slow cooker.

2. Add the garlic to the pan and sauté for 1 minute, then add the peanut butter, soy sauce, sugar, lemon juice, molasses, and cayenne pepper, scraping up the brown bits and stirring with a whisk. Add the water to the pan, stir, and pour the mixture over the lamb in the crock. Cover and cook on LOW for 6 to 8 hours.

3. At the end of the cooking time, stir in the peanuts and cilantro. Season with salt and pepper. Serve hot.

·· Slow Cooker Tip: Make-Ahead Meals ··

Using your freezer in conjunction with slow cooker cooking is a practical option. There is a whole school of thought that believes that if you make one meal, you should make enough at the same time to freeze a second meal. Make-ahead main dishes are not a new concept. With available freezer space, you can easily cook double the amount of a favorite dish and package the extras for a future meal. You will notice that many of the yields say "serves 2 with leftovers." The recipes herein, especially the soups, chilies, and braises, are often designed for a second meal.

Stews and meat braises are easy to freeze and retain their just-cooked qualities. Pasta sauces and lasagna are very popular. To save time, make pasta sauces ahead and freeze them in appropriate portions. Then all you have to do is cook the pasta and reheat the sauce. For stews and casseroles, plan to reheat them in the oven or microwave rather than the slow cooker, since the food will not heat up as fast as it should in the cooker. The only foods that are really bad for freezing are raw potatoes, cooked soft vegetables like summer squash, cream sauces, and hard-cooked eggs or fish. I also avoid freezing veal, since it is so lean, and risotto (plain steamed rice can be frozen nicely, though) and polenta. I don't freeze cooked poultry on the bone. I shred meats like chicken, turkey, and large cuts of meat in sauce so they are ready to serve when defrosted and take up less freezer space.

For freezer storage, collect plastic freezer containers in various sizes, to accommodate different amounts of food. You may also use heavy-duty zipper-top plastic freezer bags for food storage.

Tagine of Lamb, Tomato, Green Beans, and Sesame

T agines are the stews of Morocco, and they are made in a glazed earthenware casserole dish with a conical lid (also called a tagine) that looks like the top of a futuristic building. The vessel was created for slow cooking on an open fire, and the stew is traditionally served with couscous to soak up the juices. The electric slow cooker is an exact replica technique-wise for modern cooks and makes a perfectly cooked tagine with far less work. Choose the leanest lamb you can find; well-trimmed leg meat is perfect. Shoulder is flavorful but often is not lean enough. ● *Serves 2*

COOKER: 3 quart
SETTING AND COOK TIME: LOW for 6 to 8 hours; green beans added after 5 hours

1½ pounds lean boneless lamb, preferably from the leg or shoulder,
    trimmed of some fat and cut into 1- to 1½-inch cubes
Salt and freshly ground black pepper to taste
2 tablespoons olive oil
1 large yellow onion, chopped
1 clove garlic, chopped
One 3-inch cinnamon stick
3 whole green cardamom pods
1 bay leaf
½ teaspoon ground cumin
¼ teaspoon dried thyme
¼ teaspoon ground ginger
¼ teaspoon ground turmeric
Pinch of cayenne pepper
¾ cup water
3 tablespoons tomato paste
2 fresh or 3 canned plum tomatoes, peeled, seeded, and chopped
¼ cup chopped fresh Italian parsley
¾ pound fresh green beans, sliced lengthwise in half
1 heaping tablespoon sesame seeds, toasted in a dry skillet until golden, for garnish

1. Pat the lamb dry with paper towels and season with salt and pepper. In a large skillet, heat the oil over medium-high heat. Add the lamb, in batches if necessary, and brown on all sides. Remove to a plate.

2. Add the onion and garlic to the pan and cook, stirring, until the onion is soft, about 5 minutes. Transfer to the slow cooker, spreading the mixture evenly over the bottom of the crock. Place the lamb on top of the onions. Scatter the cinnamon stick, cardamom pods, and bay leaf over the lamb. If you wish, tie them into a small square of cheesecloth so you can remove them easily before serving. Add the cumin, thyme, ginger, turmeric, cayenne pepper, water, tomato paste, tomatoes, and parsley to the crock. Cover and cook on LOW for 5 hours.

3. At 5 hours, bring a small pot of salted water to a boil and blanch the green beans until nearly tender but still firm, about 3 minutes. Add the beans to the crock. Cover and cook for another 1 to 3 hours, until the meat is fork-tender.

4. Before serving, remove the cinnamon stick, bay leaf, and, if desired, the cardamom pods. Season with salt and pepper and serve hot, sprinkled with the sesame seeds.

Lamb Stew Agrodolce

ere is a gloriously simple and nourishing stew, an Italian-style sweet and sour sauce with lamb. Serve the stew over wide noodles such as pappardelle, with a tart green salad on the side. ● *Serves 2*

COOKER: 1½ to 3 quart
SETTING AND COOK TIME: LOW for 6 to 8 hours

1½ **pounds lamb shoulder or leg of lamb, trimmed of excess fat and cut into 1- to 2-inch pieces**
Salt and freshly ground black or white pepper to taste
2 tablespoons olive oil
¾ **cup water**
⅓ **cup red wine vinegar**
3 tablespoons tomato paste
2 teaspoons sugar

Season the lamb with salt and pepper. Warm the olive oil in a large sauté pan over high heat. Add the lamb, in batches if necessary, and brown quickly on all sides, about 5 minutes. Using a slotted spoon, transfer to the slow cooker. Add the water, vinegar, tomato paste, and sugar to the crock. Cover and cook on LOW for 6 to 8 hours, until the lamb is fork-tender. Serve hot.

Round Bone Lamb Chops
with Mushrooms and Sweet Peppers

I found some shoulder lamb chops in the meat case and wondered what to do with them, since they are so delicious slow cooked. Cookbook author Joyce Goldstein, in her book *Italian Slow and Savory* (Chronicle Books, 2004), recommends lamb with a combination of mushrooms and sweet bell peppers. I was not disappointed, and here is a tasty little stew. I let some hot rice soak up the flavorful juices. ○ *Serves 2*

COOKER: 1½ to 3 quart
SETTING AND COOK TIME: HIGH for 3½ to 4 hours

2 round bone shoulder lamb chops (about 1 pound), trimmed of visible fat
2 large shallots, sliced
1 teaspoon chopped fresh rosemary or oregano
4 tablespoons freshly squeezed lemon juice
¼ cup olive oil
1 medium-size red bell pepper, seeded and cut lengthwise into wide strips
Salt and freshly ground black or white pepper to taste
¼ pound brown mushrooms, such as porcini or portobello, quartered
2 to 4 lemon wedges for serving

1. Place the lamb chops, half of the shallots, the rosemary, 3 tablespoons of the lemon juice, and the olive oil in a zipper-top plastic bag. Marinate in the refrigerator for at least 3 hours or overnight.

2. Spray the inside of the crock with nonstick cooking spray. Place the pepper slices in the bottom of the crock and place the lamb chops (side by side if possible; otherwise, overlapping) with their marinade on top. Lay the remaining half of the shallots over the top. Sprinkle with salt and pepper, and drizzle the remaining 1 tablespoon of lemon juice over the top. Top with the mushrooms. Cover and cook on HIGH for 3½ to 4 hours, until the lamb is fork-tender.

3. Add salt and pepper and serve hot with the lemon wedges.

Lamb Chops in Beer

Beer acts like wine in a marinade for meat: It tenderizes as well as adds a rich flavor. Use a mild-flavored beer here rather than a dark beer or ale. If you want to thicken the sauce before serving, knead together 1 tablespoon butter and 1 tablespoon flour, and stir it in after removing the chops from the crock. Look for some nice meaty shoulder chops; a butcher shop will trim off the excess fat for you. ○ *Serves 2*

COOKER: 3 quart
SETTING AND COOK TIME: HIGH for 3½ to 4 hours

1 medium-size onion, thickly sliced
2 medium-size carrots, thickly sliced
2 red or white new potatoes, cut into wedges
1 clove garlic, crushed
2 tablespoons chopped fresh Italian parsley
¼ teaspoon chopped fresh thyme
2 lamb shoulder chops (about 1 pound)
2 tablespoons all-purpose flour
Salt and freshly ground black or white pepper to taste
1½ tablespoons olive oil
1 plum tomato, seeded and chopped
⅔ cup beer, such as lager or pilsner

1. Spray the inside of the crock with nonstick cooking spray. Combine the onion, carrots, potatoes, garlic, parsley, and thyme in the crock. Sprinkle the chops with the flour and season with salt and pepper.

2. In a large skillet, heat the oil over medium-high heat. Add the chops and cook until brown, 2 to 3 minutes. Place them in the crock, laying them side by side. Add the tomato and pour the beer over the top. Cover and cook on HIGH for 3½ to 4 hours, until the meat is fork-tender. Serve hot.

Lamb Riblets with Honey and Chipotle

L amb riblets are the bones off the premium rib chops. They are available from butcher shops that cut up their own meat. The bones are not Frenched, leaving a small, long strip of delicious meat. You can dust the bones with a fine herb mixture if you like extra flavor; my friend Jesse Cool likes garam masala with some fruit salsa. You could even use a salt-free herb blend, either with Italian herbs or dill. The idea for combining the honey, soy sauce, and chipotle powder comes from One Midtown Kitchen in Atlanta, but I've added some chunky vegetables, citrus, and salsa. This is one of those eat-with-your-hands, suck-the-meat-off-the-bones kind of suppers. ○ *Serves 2*

COOKER: 3 quart
SETTING AND COOK TIME: HIGH for about 2 hours

1 small white onion, sliced
1 clove garlic, minced
2 pounds lamb riblets, cut into sections of 4 ribs each (about 20 spareribs)
Salt and freshly ground black or white pepper to taste
½ cup honey
¼ cup low-sodium soy sauce
1¼ teaspoons chipotle paste (see page 119)
¼ cup chunky fresh salsa
2 strips lemon or lime zest
1 bunch green onions, sliced, for garnish

1. Rub the inside of the crock with olive oil. Place the onion and garlic in the bottom of the slow cooker. Arrange the riblets on top and sprinkle with salt and pepper.

2. Combine the honey, soy sauce, and chile paste in a small bowl; heat in the microwave to melt honey. Pour over the ribs and add the salsa and strips of lemon zest to the crock. Make sure all the ribs get coated with the sauce. Cover and cook on HIGH for about 2 hours. Serve hot, sprinkled with the green onions.

Baby Legs of Lamb Braised
with Shallots and Vinegar

For your first foray into cooking lamb shanks, try this recipe. Lamb shanks are like little baby legs of lamb, and they are typically made for a group or for a special meal. No more. Here you can make 1 or 2 shanks as efficiently as you would 4 or 6, and have a great, satisfying meal for pennies. I love assertive red wine vinegars, especially Merlot wine vinegar or fig red wine vinegar (available at www.cuisineperel.com). If you are a winery visitor, pick up a house vinegar along with your special wines, as most wineries make vinegar too. You will have some nice, savory cooking liquid, so serve this right out of the crock over Rice and Vermicelli Pilaf (page 217) or noodles. ● *Serves 2*

COOKER: 3 quart
SETTINGS AND COOK TIMES: HIGH for 5 hours, then LOW for 2 to 3 hours

2 lamb shanks (about 2 pounds), external fat trimmed and
    tight membrane pierced with the tip of a knife
Salt and freshly ground black pepper to taste
2 tablespoons olive oil
3 large shallots, coarsely chopped
½ cup chicken broth, canned or homemade (see page 17), or beef broth
3 tablespoons red wine vinegar

1. Wash and dry the shanks and season with salt and pepper. In a large skillet, heat the oil over medium-high heat. Add the lamb and cook until it is golden brown on all sides, 5 to 7 minutes. Place the shanks in the slow cooker, laying them side by side. Add the shallots, broth, and vinegar to the crock. Season with salt and pepper. Cover and cook on HIGH for 5 hours.

2. Reduce the heat to LOW and cook for 2 to 3 hours longer, until the lamb is tender when pierced with a fork and falling off the bone.

3. Transfer the lamb to dinner plates. Pour the juices into a pitcher or bowl and skim off the fat. Serve immediately.

•• Slow Cooker Tip: Slow Cooking with Wine ••

"A glass for the pot" is one of my cooking mantras. I rely a lot on the use of wine and spirits in my recipes. Wine is one of the world's most common beverages, along with beer and tea. It is remarkably compatible with food, not only as an accompaniment but also as a highly versatile ingredient, since it blends so nicely with a myriad of foods. It has become a staple of mine, and can be added either at the beginning of the cooking process or at the end.

When you add wine at the beginning of cooking, the sour alcohol taste will burn off and leave the delicious flavor elements; if added at the end of cooking, the taste of the "raw" wine will basically remain. Wine is often used as a marinade, as it is a great tenderizer, and then is added to the slow cooker to make the sauce. Wine adds acidity, usually permeating the ingredients, and after cooking ends up giving depth to a dish.

Alcohol comes to a boil at 172°F, so the alcohol will begin to evaporate equally efficiently on the LOW as well as the HIGH slow cooker heat settings. After a mere 10 minutes on the LOW simmer, you will have a unique and rich vinous flavor that will create the depth and character many dishes need to taste best.

There are rules for adding wine to your stews and braises. First, never, ever use a wine for cooking that you would find unsuitable for drinking. Ditto for those "cooking wines" that can ruin a stew fast. Slow cooking concentrates the qualities of the wine, and you will notice all sorts of flavors that can add up to either wonderful and rich or artificial and cloying. But you don't have to use anything expensive or rare for cooking either, unless you want to. There is a gigantic world in between from which to choose, so worry not.

Red wine generally gives a stronger flavor to food than white. Leftover opened bottles of red wine are great to use in cooking. Even if an open bottle of red has sat for weeks on your counter and turned a bit, it will still make your braised daube of beef sing. Cooks often first choose what they want to drink with their dinner, then opt for a cheaper version for the pot. This works well if you are drinking an expensive import; then just substitute a domestic version of that wine. Basic reds can include Zinfandel, Merlot, Pinot Noir, Chianti, and Cabernet Sauvignon.

White wine should be used more quickly after it has been opened, within a few days if it has been refrigerated. After that it is a throwaway, since it is more perishable. Leftover champagne works great even though it will go flat. If you use a freshly opened sparkling wine or champagne, expect that the effervescence will fade and the liquid will act quite like a white wine. Dry table wines can be used for the most part interchangeably in recipes, but never substitute a sweet dessert wine (like port, mead, or cream sherry) for a dry wine; you will ruin your dish. Basic whites are Riesling, Sauvignon Blanc, Soave, Chenin Blanc, and Gerwürztraminer. I also like vermouth, dry sherry, and dry Marsala, which are more complex and heavier than regular white wine. You can also stock some mirin, the Japanese rice wine, and Shaoxing, Chinese rice wine.

Lamb Shanks with Chickpeas, Cinnamon, and Cumin

L amb shanks taste really good with chickpeas and this combination of sweet and savory spices. These shanks do not need to be browned before going into the slow cooker. ● *Serves 2*

COOKER: 3 quart

SETTINGS AND COOK TIMES: HIGH for 5 hours, then LOW for 2 to 3 hours; chickpeas and cherries added after 4 hours

1 medium-size yellow onion, chopped

2 lamb shanks (about 2 pounds), external fat trimmed and
  tight membrane pierced with the tip of a knife

Salt and freshly ground black pepper to taste

¼ teaspoon ground cinnamon

¼ teaspoon ground cumin

½ cup chicken broth, canned or homemade (see page 17)

One 15.5-ounce can chickpeas, rinsed and drained

⅔ cup dried sweet or tart cherries

Juice of 1 small lemon

1. Place the onion in the slow cooker. Wash and dry the shanks and lay them side by side on top of the onion. Season with salt and pepper, then sprinkle with the cinnamon and cumin. Pour in the chicken broth. Cover and cook on HIGH for 4 hours.

2. At 4 hours, add the chickpeas and cherries, then drizzle the lemon juice over the beans and meat. Cover and continue cooking on HIGH for another hour.

3. Reduce the heat setting to LOW and cook for 2 to 3 hours longer, until the lamb is tender when pierced with a fork and falling off the bone.

4. Transfer the lamb to dinner plates, then serve the beans with a slotted spoon. Pour the juices into a pitcher or bowl and skim off the fat. Serve the juices on the side.

King of the Slow Cooker
Beef and Veal

It seems like beef was made for stewing and braising in the slow cooker. Want to transform a tough piece of meat into a luscious fork-tender dinner? Braise it in the slow cooker. Brown it to give it some color (or not!) and to start building flavor in the pot. Add aromatics and vegetables, a bit of liquid, and you've got it. The slow cooker does the rest, and you can walk away and do other things while your dinner braises nicely on the counter with no fuss.

Take a walk down your meat aisle. You will notice that you look first at certain familiar areas for the types of beef you eat most and are most used to preparing, like the prime cuts of steak, which are great for the broiler or grill but would toughen mercilessly if slow cooked, and large hunks of roast like bottom rounds, which are much too big for cooking for two. Take the time to look at the cuts of beef you may never have chosen before or may have passed over because you didn't know how to cook them. Also notice that these are the least expensive, more muscley and fatty cuts. Even with all the bad press on fat in the diet, remember that some fat is necessary for proper tenderness, juiciness, and flavor in the slow cooker.

The tougher cuts are the ones that are perfect for braising in the slow cooker and end up delivering the most flavor. They include the shank, brisket, chuck roast, flank steak, skirt steak, and short ribs. While these cuts start out tough, the long, moist cooking time produces the most tender, luscious, deeply flavored dishes. As the liquid simmers, it turns to steam, rising and hitting the lid, then dripping back down. As it continues going up and falling down, it picks up flavor from the meat and other ingredients, knitting them into a complex sauce. The fibers in the meat slowly melt, making the meat tender.

When choosing a cut of beef, look for slightly moist meat with a light cherry red to red-brown hue, a clean smell, tight grain, marbled intramuscular fat (flecks of fat throughout the meat), and white external fat. Check expiration dates before buying packaged meat, and look for USDA Choice grade meats, as they are the most juicy and flavorful. Often the lower grade, Select, while a lot leaner than Choice, is also fine for stewing and braising. Shop at a reliable supermarket or butcher shop and do not hesitate to ask questions; fine cooks value the advice of a knowledgeable meat cutter or butcher, and that butcher should be happy to give the advice.

Chuck roasts, often sold as a flat hunk rather than a tied round, will cook up moist and tender, never tough and stringy, in the slow cooker. This is the cut to use for portioning your own stew meat. You can also use beef cheeks or shin meat for stews.

Veal is considered a luxury meat but is treated in the same manner as beef in the slow cooker. There are a multitude of wonderful recipes using it, since it is so well suited to braising due to the collagen that cooks down into natural gelatin, giving lovely body and texture to stews. Despite this, veal remains the leanest of meats. Veal also takes to all sorts of spices, vegetables, and aromatic braising liquids because of its complementary delicate taste.

There are two types of veal available today—formula-fed, which is characterized by its pale pink appearance, and grass-fed, which has a more ruddy and flavorful meat. Both types can be used interchangeably, although the darker meat is a bit tougher. Look for veal that is firm, dense, and uniform in color, with creamy white fat and no marbling.

Veal stews, cut from the chuck, breast, and shoulder, are a favorite in the slow cooker. Blade shoulder roasts are really good for cutting up into stew meat, as well as being the most economical. Don't overcook veal, though; it will dry out easily. Veal shanks, a popular restaurant cut of veal from the back legs, cook up almost as silky as they are tender. They are often cut in one or two places to expose the marrow, a delicacy in osso buco.

Food Safety

As always, be aware of keeping all food preparation surfaces clean and free from bacterial contamination by washing your hands, counters, cutting boards, and knives with warm soapy water. *E. coli* is the pathogen most commonly associated with beef, living on the surface, but proper cooking will ensure no cross-contamination, and the heat process will kill any existing bacteria. Never eat raw meat, and freeze any meat that is to be stored longer than 3 days. Thaw all meat in the refrigerator or microwave, not at room temperature.

Merlot Beef Ragoût

Here is a wonderfully classic beef stew adapted from a recipe simply called Beef en Casserole, which was once on the menu at the now-defunct Russian Tea Room in New York City. I use a quality Merlot, since the great flavor of the red wine is highlighted in the simplicity of this stew. The browning of the meat is important for this dish, so don't skip it for lack of time. I love this stew with Spaetzle Dumplings (page 225). The restaurant served it with fluffy rice pilaf and a green salad on the side. Save the extra for dinner the next day, or cool and freeze for a future meal. Of course, if you were dining on this in the Russian Tea Room, you would have a starter of beluga caviar on toast and a shot of icy cold vodka.

○ *Serves 2 with leftovers*

COOKER: 1½ to 3 quart
SETTING AND COOK TIME: LOW for 7 to 8 hours;
   optional to cook on HIGH for last 45 minutes

1¾ pounds lean, boneless beef stew meat, chuck or bottom round,
   trimmed of fat and cut into 1½-inch chunks
1 teaspoon salt
½ teaspoon freshly ground black pepper
3 tablespoons olive oil
2 medium-size onions, chopped
1 clove garlic, crushed
One 14.5-ounce can diced peeled tomatoes, drained
1 cup dry red wine, such as Merlot

1. Sprinkle the cubes of beef with salt and pepper. In a large sauté pan over medium-high heat, heat the oil until very hot. Add half of the beef and brown on all sides, 3 to 4 minutes. Transfer to the slow cooker. Repeat the browning with the remaining beef.

2. Add the onions to the skillet and brown slightly over medium-high heat; add the garlic and cook just for 15 seconds or so, then add the onions and garlic to the crock.

3. Pour the tomatoes and wine into the sauté pan and raise the heat to high. Stir constantly while bringing to a boil, scraping up the browned bits accumulated on the bottom of the pan. Pour into the crock. Cover and cook on LOW for 7 to 8 hours, until the meat is tender.

4. During the last 45 minutes of cooking, check the consistency. If the juices are too thin for you, increase the heat to HIGH and leave the cover off, letting some moisture evaporate. Serve hot.

• • Slow Cooker Tip: Prepping Ahead • •

If you are pressed for time, prep your ingredients the day before cooking by chopping vegetables and storing them separately in sealed containers or plastic storage bags. Cover cut potatoes with water to prevent discoloring. Ground meat can be browned and refrigerated overnight as long as it is fully cooked (browned roasts, cubed meat, and poultry all need to be prepped just before cooking for safety, since browning them does not fully cook them). Fresh poultry pieces can be quickly grilled on an outdoor grill, then immediately frozen for later use. Ingredients, except for meat and poultry, can be assembled in the crock and refrigerated, covered, overnight; in the morning, you just insert the crock into the housing and turn on the machine.

Baby Beef Stew
with Grappa and Olives

ere is a little beef stew just for two with no leftovers. Buy the package of already cut stew meat, nice and fresh, of course, and stash half of it in the freezer for the next stew. The combination of pancetta and coppa ham (you can get those in an Italian deli) really makes this stew taste soooo good. The splash of grappa can be replaced with some regular brandy if you don't have grappa on your shelf. I use my 1½-quart slow cooker for this stew and serve it over noodles or rice. This recipe was inspired by Bruce Aidells. ○ *Serves 2*

COOKER: 1½ to 3 quart
SETTING AND COOK TIME: LOW for 7 to 8 hours; olives added during last hour

¾ **pound lean, boneless beef stew meat (chuck or bottom round)**
Salt and freshly ground black or white pepper to taste
Pinch of paprika
¼ **teaspoon dried thyme or basil**
1 tablespoon olive oil
3 slices coppa, chopped
2 slices pancetta, diced
2 tablespoons all-purpose flour
½ **medium-size onion, chopped**
1 clove garlic, crushed
½ **cup canned diced tomatoes, drained**
½ **bay leaf**
½ **cup beef broth**
2 tablespoons grappa or brandy
¼ **cup whole pitted black olives in brine, drained**

1. Place the cubes of beef in a bowl and sprinkle with the salt, pepper, paprika, and thyme. Refrigerate to marinate for at least 2 hours or overnight.

2. In a medium sauté pan over medium heat, heat the oil until very hot. Add the coppa and pancetta and cook until the pancetta is crispy, 4 minutes. Remove with a slotted spoon and drain on paper towels.

3. Toss the seasoned beef with the flour and add to the hot pan; brown on all sides, 3 to 4 minutes.

4. Spray the inside of the crock with nonstick cooking spray and add the onion and garlic. Add the beef and the pancetta-coppa mixture. Add the tomatoes and bay leaf. If you are feeling ambitious, add the wine to the pan and bring to a boil to deglaze, then add to the crock, or else just add to the crock. Add the broth and grappa to the crock. Cover and cook on LOW for 7 to 8 hours, until the meat is fork-tender.

5. Add the olives during the last hour of cooking. Serve hot.

Baby Beef Stew Classico

I thought I had better include a down-home-style, nothing-fancy, lottsa-veggies, mom's beef stew here, since I use the 1½-quart slow cooker so often to make this. I cut my own stew meat from a boneless chuck roast, and it tastes so great. If you have never cut your own stew meat, I recommend you do it here with a small amount. You will get the reward of tender, juicy, and top-notch flavor. Get a nice 3-pound chuck roast, lean and fresh cut, and put it on your cutting board. From your knife set, choose a long-bladed, sharp knife used for boning. Cut the meat into three equal portions; freeze two portions for another stew or for pot roast. Then cut the last pound portion into cubes and proceed; it is that easy. Many people just toss the meat into the cooker, but a good stew needs the quick initial browning to caramelize the meat; the end flavor will reflect it. Serve this over noodles or rice, or with a nice crusty bread. ○ *Serves 2*

COOKER: 1½ to 3 quart

SETTING AND COOK TIME: HIGH for 4 to 5 hours, or LOW for 7 to 8 hours; peas added during last 30 minutes

1 pound lean, boneless chuck roast, trimmed of fat and cut into 1½-inch chunks

Salt and freshly ground black or white pepper to taste

1 tablespoon olive oil

1 small yellow onion, chopped

¼ pound baby carrots

1 small parsnip, peeled and diced

6 ounces baby red potatoes, halved or quartered

1½ cups beef broth

½ cup dry red wine

2 tablespoons tomato paste

4 sun-dried tomatoes packed in oil, drained and chopped

½ teaspoon dried thyme or marjoram

1½ tablespoons unsalted butter, softened

1½ tablespoons all-purpose flour

¼ cup frozen petit peas, thawed

1. Sprinkle the cubes of beef with some salt and pepper. In a medium-size sauté pan over medium heat, heat the oil until very hot. Add the meat cubes and brown on all sides, 4 to 5 minutes.

2. Spray the crock with nonstick cooking spray and add the onion, carrots, parsnip, and potatoes. Add the meat, broth, wine, tomato paste, sun-dried tomatoes, and thyme; mix well. Cover and cook on HIGH for 4 to 5 hours (or LOW for 7 to 8 hours), until the meat is fork-tender.

3. When there is about 30 minutes of cooking time left, knead the butter and flour together in a small bowl with a fork. Add the butter-flour ball (known as a *beurre manié*) to the crock and stir until melted. Add the peas to the crock. Cover and cook another 30 minutes. Season to taste and serve hot.

•• Slow Cooker Tip: Root Vegetables and Timing ••

After concocting your first beef stew or turkey stew in the slow cooker, you might have experienced how long root vegetables take to cook. To cook properly, root vegetables (carrots, parsnips, turnips, sweet potatoes, and, most particularly, potatoes of all varieties) must be cut into thin slices or diced into small cubes no larger than 1 inch square. This will ensure that the vegetables cook in approximately the same amount of time as the meat. If perchance your vegetables are not cooked and your meat is fork-tender, then remove the meat with a slotted spoon and cover to keep warm. Adjust the heat setting to HIGH and cook the vegetables until cooked to your desired degree of tenderness, testing at 30-minute intervals. When they are done, return the meat to the hot stew to reheat briefly before serving.

Beef Tagine with Dried Mango and Raisins

he slow cooker is a dream for transforming and adapting the classic tagines of North Africa into an easy affair. The flavor combinations are exotic, and I could not resist adding the dried mango here; you can substitute dried apricots if you cannot find dried mango. Spicy-hot harissa paste is a combination of chile peppers, black pepper, cinnamon, and cloves; it is available in cans and jars in ethnic markets. Serve this with a plain couscous, and place on an oval platter to serve. I like a small bowl of plain yogurt for dolloping on top as well, and a grated raw carrot salad on the side. ○ *Serves 2 with leftovers*

COOKER: 3 quart
SETTING AND COOK TIME: LOW for 7 to 8 hours;
 mango, raisins, and harissa added after 5 hours

1 teaspoon ground ginger

1 teaspoon ground coriander

Pinch of saffron threads

¼ teaspoon salt

Freshly ground black pepper to taste

3 tablespoons olive oil

1¾ pounds lean, boneless beef stew meat, chuck or bottom round,
 trimmed of fat and cut into 1-inch chunks

1 large yellow onion, halved and sliced

1 clove garlic, minced

1 tablespoon all-purpose or whole wheat pastry flour

1⅓ cups vegetable broth, canned or homemade (see page 18)

1 cinnamon stick

⅔ cup coarsely chopped dried mango

½ cup golden raisins

1 teaspoon harissa

3 tablespoons chopped fresh Italian parsley, for garnish

1 tablespoon sesame seeds, toasted in a dry skillet, for garnish

About 1 teaspoon orange flower water for garnish

1. Combine the ginger, coriander, saffron, salt, and pepper in a medium-size bowl and add 2 tablespoons of the olive oil. Add the beef cubes and rub the mixture into the beef with your fingertips.

2. In a large sauté pan over medium-high heat, heat the remaining 1 tablespoon oil until very hot. Add the beef and brown on all sides, 3 to 4 minutes. Transfer to the slow cooker. Add the onion and garlic to the skillet and brown slightly over medium heat for 3 minutes, then sprinkle with the flour and cook for 1 minute. Add the vegetable broth to the skillet and bring to a boil. Pour into the crock over the meat and add the cinnamon stick. Cover and cook on LOW for 5 hours.

3. Add the mango, raisins, and harissa, and stir to combine. Cover and cook for 2 to 3 more hours. Add more salt and pepper, if desired.

4. Serve hot on a small platter with the parsley, toasted sesame seeds, and orange flower water sprinkled over the top.

Lou's Beef Stifatho

(L)ou is my friend and fellow cookbook writer Lou Pappas. She is in the know about Greek cooking, and here is a simply wonderful beef stew called a stifado, or *stifatho* in Greek (originally the name of the variety of onion used in the stew), with a few twists, like whole cloves and pickling spices. This beef stew has stood the test of time, and Lou calls it one of her great recipes. I think you will agree. The recipe is from her book *Extra-Special Crockery Pot Recipes* (Bristol Publishing), which was originally published 30 years ago, but last revised in 1994. That puts Lou writing that cookbook during what I call the dark ages of slow cooker cooking, when there were many limitations on the appliance. I asked Lou what to serve with her stew. She says, "This calls for a classic Greek dinner: country salad (with tomatoes, cucumbers, and feta) and rice pilaf. You could add steamed broccoli, and then for dessert, just fresh seasonal fruit or strawberries drizzled with honey. Of course, I have a fondness for homemade ice cream, something like lavender ice cream, or if without lavender, then with Grand Marnier or framboise." ● *Serves 2 with leftovers*

COOKER: 3 quart
SETTING AND COOK TIME: LOW for 7 to 8 hours

2 tablespoons olive oil
2½ pounds lean, boneless beef stew meat, chuck or bottom round,
    trimmed of fat and cut into 1-inch chunks
1 teaspoon whole mixed pickling spice, tied in a cheesecloth bag with 4 whole cloves
3 cloves garlic, minced
1 pound frozen whole baby onions, thawed
2 tablespoons firmly packed brown sugar
½ cup dry red wine
½ cup water
4 tablespoons tomato paste
¼ cup red wine vinegar
Salt and freshly ground black pepper to taste

1. In a large sauté pan over medium-high heat, heat the oil until very hot. Add half of the beef and brown on all sides, 3 to 4 minutes. Transfer to the slow cooker. Repeat the browning with the remaining beef. Add the spice bag and garlic to the crock.

2. Add the onions and brown sugar to the skillet and brown slightly over medium heat for 3 to 5 minutes (they will become glazed), then add to the crock.

3. Add the wine, water, tomato paste, and vinegar to the skillet and stir for a few minutes to scrape up the drippings. Pour into the crock. Season with salt and pepper. Cover and cook on LOW for 7 to 8 hours, until fork-tender.

4. Remove and discard the spice bag. If you wish, increase the heat to HIGH and leave the cover off for a few minutes, to slightly reduce the juices. Serve hot.

Barbecue Braised Brisket with Butter Beans

I adore this recipe, especially during the winter. The butter beans, a favorite of my mother's and always included in every baked bean recipe she makes, are an unusual touch. Always keep one bottle of your favorite barbecue sauce in the pantry for culinary inspirations like this one. This recipe is best made the day before, if you can wait that long to eat it. ○ *Serves 2 with leftovers*

COOKER: 3 quart
SETTING AND COOK TIME: LOW for 10 to 12 hours

½ cup barbecue sauce of your choice
⅓ cup ginger ale
1 tablespoon brown sugar
1 tablespoon honey
2 medium-size yellow onions, sliced
2½ pounds beef brisket, trimmed of as much fat as possible and blotted dry
Salt and freshly ground black pepper to taste
One 15-ounce can butter (lima) beans, drained

1. In a small bowl, combine the barbecue sauce, ginger ale, brown sugar, and honey.

2. Place the onions in the bottom of the slow cooker. Lay the meat on top, fitting snugly and seasoning with salt and pepper. If the meat is too big to lay flat in your cooker, cut it in half and stack the pieces one atop the other.

3. Pour the sauce over the meat. Cover and cook on LOW for 10 to 12 hours. If you plan to eat this right away, add the butter beans during the last hour to heat through. Otherwise, leave them out.

4. You may serve immediately, slicing the meat against the grain. Or place the meat on a piece of foil and cool before refrigerating. Refrigerate the sauce separately. When ready to serve, degrease the cold sauce and discard the hardened piece of fat. Add the butter beans to the sauce, and reheat the brisket in the onions and sauce.

Espresso-Braised Pot Roast with Balsamic Vinegar

You will love the subtle, aromatic combination of beef in coffee and rich balsamic vinegar. Beef chuck roast is well marbled, and while it is not the leanest cut, don't shy away from using it, as it cooks up nice and tender. You can make this the day before and refrigerate it overnight. Keep the pepper grinder on the table so you can add some at serving time. ○ *Serves 2 with leftovers*

COOKER: 3 quart
SETTING AND COOK TIME: LOW for 8 to 9 hours

1½ pounds boneless chuck roast, trimmed of as much fat as possible and blotted dry
¼ teaspoon salt, or to taste
Freshly ground black pepper to taste
1 large yellow onion, thinly sliced
1 tablespoon olive oil
⅓ cup strong brewed coffee or espresso
2 tablespoons balsamic vinegar
1½ tablespoons cornstarch mixed with 1½ tablespoons water

1. Rub all sides of the roast with the salt and pepper. Place the onion in the bottom of the slow cooker and toss with the olive oil. Place the meat on top of the onion. Add the coffee and vinegar. Cover and cook on LOW for 8 to 9 hours, until tender.

2. Transfer the beef to a cutting board, tent with foil, and let rest for about 10 minutes. Meanwhile, skim the fat from the braising liquid in the crock. Transfer the liquid to a saucepan and bring to a boil over medium-high heat. Add the cornstarch mixture and cook, whisking, until the gravy thickens slightly, about 1 minute. Carve the beef and serve hot with the gravy.

Old-Fashioned Meatloaf

Many cooks swear that the meatloaf that emerges from the slow cooker is better than any that comes out of a traditional oven. I agree. It is so moist and easy to slice. Leftover meatloaf tastes great too, since the flavors marry and the texture firms up for a nice sandwich. Please note that the directions include a technique for removing the tender freeform loaf without breaking it by making a sort of aluminum foil cradle. This was inspired by a recipe from my dear friend, an incredible cook and prodigious food writer, Rick Rodgers. ○ *Serves 2 with leftovers*

COOKER: 1½ or 3 quart

SETTING AND COOK TIME: HIGH for 3 to 4 hours

1½ **pounds ground chuck or meatloaf mix of equal parts ground beef, pork, and veal**

⅔ **cup quick-cooking rolled oats**

1 **egg, beaten**

⅓ **cup ketchup**

1 **tablespoon Worcestershire sauce**

1 **tablespoon minced onion or shallot**

3 **tablespoons grated carrot**

1 **teaspoon salt**

Freshly ground black pepper to taste

½ **cup ketchup or tomato chili sauce for topping**

·· Slow Cooker Tip: HIGHs and LOWs ··

Many cooks like to cook on HIGH for 1 hour to heat up the contents of the pot more quickly, then adjust to LOW if the recipe is written to be cooked on a LOW setting.

---

1. Place the ground meat, oats, and egg in a large mixing bowl. Add the ketchup, Worcestershire sauce, onion, carrot, salt, and pepper. Using your hands or a large fork, mix gently but thoroughly, being careful not to compact the meat. Shape the meat mixture into a mounded oval or round loaf, depending on the shape of your cooker.

2. Make a foil "cradle" that will help you easily remove the meatloaf from the cooker when it is done. Tear a sheet of heavy-duty aluminum foil that is about 14 inches long. Fold in half lengthwise, then in half again lengthwise to make a strip about 3 inches wide. Place the foil strip into the crock lengthwise, pushing into opposite sides to secure. The edges of the foil strip will come up the sides of the crock; they don't need to come out the top. Center the meatloaf in the crock, on top of the strip, and spread the ketchup on top. Cover and cook on HIGH for 3 to 4 hours, until a meat thermometer inserted into the center of the meatloaf reads 160° to 165°F.

3. To serve, simply grasp the foil handles and lift the meatloaf up and out of the crock onto a cutting board or serving plate. Push the meatloaf off the foil strip and discard the foil. Slice the meatloaf and serve hot, or refrigerate and serve cold the next day.

Short Ribs of Beef with Zinfandel and Balsamic Vinegar

orget about all that messy work browning the ribs first in a Dutch oven. The slow cooker makes these ribs every bit as good, with no splattering with that first step. The beef ribs are meaty and juicy. Serve with creamy polenta and steamed vegetables or a big salad. ○ *Serves 2*

COOKER: 3 quart
SETTING AND COOK TIME: LOW for 7 to 8 hours

One 8-ounce can tomato sauce
⅔ cup red wine, preferably Zinfandel
1 large shallot, finely chopped
2½ tablespoons balsamic vinegar
1 tablespoon Dijon mustard
4 drops hot sauce, such as Tabasco
½ teaspoon salt
3 pounds beef short ribs, cut into serving pieces of 3 to 4 ribs

1. Combine the tomato sauce, wine, shallot, vinegar, mustard, hot sauce, and salt in a small bowl and mix until smooth.

2. Arrange the rib portions in the slow cooker and pour the sauce over them; if you have a round cooker, stack the ribs. Cover and cook on LOW for 7 to 8 hours, until the meat is tender and starts to separate from the bone.

3. Transfer the ribs to a platter and set aside. Cool the sauce until the fat congeals on the surface, then remove and discard the fat. When ready to serve, return the ribs to the sauce and reheat in a 300°F oven until hot. Serve immediately.

Cabernet Short Ribs of Beef with Apricots

S hort ribs of beef, once a hassle to cook and often overlooked at the meat counter, are just glorious in the slow cooker—and easy. They are so flavorful because they are the rib portion just below the prime rib. It makes a luscious tasty meal for two with mashed potatoes and a vegetable like steamed broccoli. Be sure to use Cabernet wine here; you want its assertive, oaky flavor. I've adapted this from a traditional stovetop-braised recipe in *Sunset* magazine. o *Serves 2*

COOKER: 3 quart
SETTING AND COOK TIME: LOW for 7 to 8 hours

1 cup Cabernet Sauvignon
1 medium-size yellow onion, chopped
2 cloves garlic, chopped
⅔ cup coarsely chopped dried apricots
1½ tablespoons Dijon mustard
1 teaspoon salt
3 pounds beef short ribs, cut into serving pieces of 3 to 4 ribs

1. Combine the wine, onion, garlic, apricots, mustard, and salt in a small bowl and mix until smooth.

2. Arrange the rib portions in the slow cooker and pour the sauce over them, making sure the onions and apricots are distributed evenly over the ribs; if you have a round cooker, stack the ribs. Cover and cook on LOW for 7 to 8 hours, until the meat is tender and starts to separate from the bone.

3. Transfer the ribs to a platter and set aside. Cool the sauce until the fat congeals on the surface, then remove and discard the fat. When ready to serve, return the ribs to the sauce and reheat in a 300°F oven until hot. Serve immediately.

Smothered Skirt Steak with Basil Sauce Fiorentino

o my sister's delight, my brother-in-law has transformed himself into a gourmet home cook by taking classes at a Sur La Table cooking school in the Seattle region. He took a class on beef given by Lynne Vea, and brought home this recipe for braised skirt steak with sweet and savory spices. It is adapted here for the slow cooker. Skirt steak, long, thin, and coarse-grained like flank steak, is flavorful and rich meat that comes off the rib cage. Once considered "low-class" and relegated to the outdoor grill, it is now the slow cook's dream, with its bit of marbled fat that translates into juicy bistro fare. One end is thinner than the other, and it is most often sold rolled up in individual portions. Make this immediately. ○ *Serves 2 with leftovers*

COOKER: 1½ to 3 quart
SETTING AND COOK TIME: LOW for 8 to 10 hours

1½ tablespoons olive oil
4 skirt steaks (about 1½ pounds total), about 1 inch thick
½ teaspoon salt
Freshly ground black pepper to taste
½ large yellow onion, chopped
1½ strips bacon, chopped
2 cloves garlic, minced
⅓ cup Chianti
⅓ cups beef broth
¼ teaspoon ground cinnamon
¼ teaspoon ground cumin
⅛ teaspoon ground cloves
¼ teaspoon dried thyme
¼ teaspoon dried savory

BASIL SAUCE FIORENTINO:

½ cup basil leaves

¼ cup coarsely chopped fresh Italian parsley

1 clove garlic

1 tablespoon capers, rinsed

2 tablespoons blanched slivered almonds or pine nuts

Squeeze of fresh lemon juice

Pinch of salt

¼ cup olive oil

2 teaspoons unsalted butter mashed with 2 teaspoons all-purpose flour (optional)

1. In a large sauté pan over medium-high heat, heat the oil until very hot. Season the beef with salt and pepper. Add two pieces of the beef and brown on all sides, about 3 minutes. Transfer to the slow cooker. Repeat with the other pieces of beef. Spoon off and discard all but 2 tablespoons of the drippings, if necessary. Add the onion and bacon and cook for 3 minutes. Add the garlic and stir a few seconds; add the mixture to the crock.

2. Add the wine to the skillet and bring to a boil, scraping up any browned bits. Pour into the crock over the meat and add the broth, cinnamon, cumin, cloves, thyme, and savory. Cover and cook on LOW for 8 to 10 hours, until fork-tender.

3. Meanwhile, to make the basil sauce, place all of the ingredients in the bowl of a food processor and pulse until smooth and pourable. Store in a covered container in the refrigerator until ready to serve.

4. Transfer the meat to a cutting board. Slice the meat and transfer to a serving platter. If you wish, you can thicken the braising liquid with 2 teaspoons butter mashed with 2 teaspoons all-purpose flour; turn to HIGH and add, stirring until thickened. Pour the braising sauce over the slices and garnish with the basil sauce.

Skirt Steak Fajitas
with Tomato-Olive Salsa

ajitas are eaten as a make-your-own-mini-burrito/soft taco and are one of the many reasons to own a slow cooker. Skirt steak is the original meat for fajitas, the name of which comes from the word *faja* or "belt" and which have been made in Texas by ranch hands since the 1930s. The meat was so tough and inexpensive that it was used as pay for the workers, who marinated it in lime juice and barbecued it outdoors. Here, you don't have to marinate the meat first, since that is automatically taken care of as the meat slow cooks. If you get one piece of skirt steak from the butcher, just cut it into two pieces. Toast your tortillas over a gas burner or lay them on an electric burner for an authentic touch. ● *Serves 2*

COOKER: 1½ to 3 quart
SETTING AND COOK TIME: LOW for 7 to 9 hours

1 tablespoon olive oil
3 tablespoons freshly squeezed lime juice
1 clove garlic, minced
½ teaspoon salt
¼ teaspoon freshly ground black pepper
3 to 4 skirt steaks (1¼ to 1½ pounds total), about 1 inch thick, or 1 piece, cut in half
1 large white onion, thinly sliced

TOMATO-OLIVE SALSA:
3 ripe plum tomatoes, seeded and chopped
3 tablespoons chopped kalamata olives
2 tablespoons olive oil
2 tablespoons chopped fresh cilantro
1 tablespoon minced red onion
2 teaspoons balsamic vinegar
Pinch of salt

4 flour tortillas, warmed, for serving

1. In a small bowl, combine the olive oil, lime juice, garlic, salt, and pepper. Lay the skirt steak pieces in the slow cooker and pour the mixture over the steak, being sure to coat all exposed surfaces well. Lay the onion over the top. Cover and cook on LOW for 7 to 9 hours, until fork-tender.

2. Meanwhile, to make the salsa, combine all the ingredients in a small bowl. Let stand at room temperature until ready to serve, or cover and refrigerate.

3. Remove the steak and onions to a serving platter, cover with foil, and let rest for 10 minutes before slicing thinly across the grain. Serve wrapped in the tortillas with lots of the salsa, and let it drip delightfully down your chin as you eat.

·· Slow Cooker Tip: Slow Cooker Timers ··

Delay timers are now available, which can be placed in an electrical outlet with the slow cooker directly plugged into them. A delay timer helps you further preschedule your cook times in cases, for example, when you have a stew that cooks for 8 hours but you will not be home for 10 hours. When using a delay timer, make sure that the ingredients are all well chilled when they go into the cooker, and set the time to start cooking within 2 hours. *Never* use delay timers with recipes that contain poultry of any type or fish. You can also buy timers that have an extra option to switch the machine to the KEEP WARM setting at the end of cooking. The Rival Smart-Pot machines can be programmed so that after the food has cooked for the designated amount of time, the pot will switch automatically to KEEP WARM.

Chinese Pepper Steak

F lank steak is one of my favorite cuts of meat, but I want to be able to prepare it in other ways than just on the outdoor grill. A relatively low-fat cut of beef, it is fantastic prepared in the slow cooker, which keeps all the juices intact. My mother was famous for her Chinese Pepper Steak, the only Asian-flavored dish she made at home in the 1960s. We always looked forward to when she would prepare it. Serve this with plain steamed rice and a simple vegetable stir-fry. ● *Serves 2*

COOKER: 3 quart
SETTING AND COOK TIME: HIGH for about 3 hours

1½ pounds flank steak, thinly sliced diagonally across the grain into ½-inch-thick slices
1 green bell pepper, stemmed, seeded, and cut into slices
One 10.5-ounce can beef consommé
¼ cup low-sodium soy sauce
1 tablespoon grated fresh ginger
1 bunch green onions, white and green parts separated and sliced
2 tablespoons cornstarch
2 tablespoons cold water or chilled mirin or Shaoxing rice wine

1. Place the meat and green pepper in the slow cooker. Add the consommé, soy sauce, ginger, and white parts only of the green onion. Cover and cook on **HIGH** for about 3 hours, until tender.

2. In a small bowl, whisk together the cornstarch and cold water; pour into the crock and stir. Cover and cook on HIGH for 10 to 15 minutes, until thickened slightly and the juices are clear. Serve immediately, garnished with the reserved sliced green onion tops.

Corned Beef and Lentils

orned beef is so delicious in the slow cooker that I had to use it in an entirely different way than just with vegetables in the style we all eat for St. Patrick's Day. Also, when you cut the meat in half, you will have the other piece in the freezer, begging to be used. I love nestling the meat into a bed of lentils, and here the tenacious cut of beef becomes meltingly tender and very hearty fare. I consider this real country-style food, especially nice in the winter when served with French bread and butter. A version of this was originally developed by food writer Cynthia Scheer for the California Culinary Academy series more than 20 years ago. ○ *Serves 2 with leftovers*

COOKER: 3 quart
SETTINGS AND COOK TIMES: HIGH for 1 hour, then LOW for 10 to 12 hours

1 cup brown lentils, rinsed and picked over
4 ounces small white boiling onions, peeled and halved
1 stalk celery, diced
4 baby carrots, diced
2 tablespoons chopped fresh Italian parsley
1 teaspoon whole mixed pickling spice, tied in a cheesecloth bag with 4 whole cloves
1 clove garlic, minced
1¼ cups hot water
¼ cup dry white wine
1 piece (1½ to 2 pounds) corned beef brisket, trimmed of all fat and rinsed in hot water
Dijon mustard for serving

1. Place the lentils, onions, celery, carrots, parsley, spice bag, garlic, hot water, and wine in the slow cooker; place the meat on top and nestle it in. If you have a round cooker and the meat is too big to lay flat in your cooker, cut it in half and stack the pieces one atop the other. Cover and cook on HIGH for 1 hour, then reduce the heat to LOW and cook for 10 to 12 hours, until the meat is fork-tender. (Check at 5 hours; if the lentils have absorbed all the water, add another ½ cup boiling water.)

2. Transfer the corned beef to a deep platter and spoon the lentils on the side. Slice the beef across the grain and serve hot, with the mustard on the side.

Corned Beef, Cabbage, and Carrots

Corned beef is one of the most popular dishes in the slow cooker because it comes out so tender. When I talk to people who prepare my slow cooker recipes, they often say the first thing they made is the corned beef, so I figured I'd better not leave it out of this book. Beef brisket is corned, which means brined, in a salt and spice mixture, an old-fashioned method of preserving before refrigeration. The meat is so tasty that it has remained a favorite. As with brisket, the piece of meat is long and flat, and easy to cut in half to serve two, with the second portion waiting in the freezer. I have also been able to find small vacuum-packed pieces suitable for serving two. ◦ *Serves 2 with leftovers*

COOKER: 3 quart
SETTINGS AND COOK TIMES: LOW for 10 to 12 hours, then HIGH for 20 to 30 minutes

2 medium-size carrots, cut on the diagonal into 2-inch chunks
1 medium-size yellow onion, cut into 6 wedges
1 piece (1½ to 2 pounds) corned beef brisket with seasoning packet,
    trimmed of all fat and rinsed in hot water
2 tablespoons dry white wine
½ of a small head of white cabbage, cut into 6 wedges,
    each secured with kitchen twine
¼ cup Dijon mustard for serving
1 recipe Horseradish Sauce for serving (recipe follows)

1. Place the carrots and onion in the bottom of the slow cooker. Lay the corned beef on top of the vegetables and sprinkle with the seasonings from the packet and the white wine. If you have a round cooker and the meat is too big to lay flat in your cooker, cut it in half and stack the pieces one atop the other. Add enough water just to cover the brisket, being careful not to fill the crock more than 1 inch from the top. Cover and cook on LOW for to 10 to 12 hours.

2. Remove the corned beef from the cooker and place in a serving casserole. Place the carrots and onion around the beef; cover with foil to keep warm. Drop the cabbage into the crock with the cooking liquid and turn the heat to HIGH. Cover and cook for 20 to 30 minutes, until the cabbage is crisp-tender when pierced with the tip of a knife.

3. Slice the beef across the grain and serve with the juices from the pot, with the mustard and the horseradish sauce, and the vegetables on the side.

Horseradish Sauce

The best part of eating corned beef is slathering it with a mildly hot horseradish sauce to titillate the taste buds with the combination of the bitter root with the sweet meat and vegetables. You can buy prepared commercial horseradish, but if you find the fresh root, you can grate your own in the food processor; be prepared, it is much hotter than the bottled. You can make this up to 1 day ahead of time.

○ *Makes about ¹/₂ cup*

¹/₄ cup mayonnaise

3 tablespoons sour cream or plain yogurt

2 to 3 tablespoons prepared horseradish

2 teaspoons rice vinegar or champagne vinegar

Pinch of salt

Combine all the ingredients in a small bowl and mix well. Cover and refrigerate until ready to serve.

Individual Pot Roasts

(I) am always eyeing the plump center-cut slices of beef shanks at the butcher's and wondering what the best way would be to cook them in the slow cooker. Here they are as individual one-to-a-person pot roasts, called *daubes* in France, in a rich vegetable sauce. This is adapted from a recipe by one of my favorite Bay Area food writers, Cynthia Scheer. Don't skip the parsley and arugula garnish at the end; it really makes the flavor and texture extra special. Be sure to get two shank slices, not one giant one, so that each diner has an individual roast.

○ *Serves 2*

COOKER: 3 quart
SETTING AND COOK TIME: LOW for 9 to 11 hours

½ teaspoon salt
¼ teaspoon freshly ground black pepper
2 tablespoons all-purpose flour
2 center-cut beef shanks (about 1¼ pounds total), at least 1 inch thick
1 tablespoon unsalted butter
1 tablespoon olive oil
4 to 6 small boiling onions, peeled
8 baby carrots
1 clove garlic, crushed
2 shallots, sliced
1 stalk celery, chopped
4 ounces fresh mushrooms of your choice, quartered
2 plum tomatoes, halved, seeded, and chopped
¼ cup dry red or white wine
1 tablespoon tomato paste
1 tablespoon Worcestershire sauce
2 tablespoons chopped fresh Italian parsley for serving
¼ bunch arugula, cut into ¼-inch ribbons, for serving

1. Place the salt, pepper, and flour in a plastic bag. Add the shanks one at a time and shake to coat. In a large sauté pan over medium-high heat, heat half of the butter and oil until very hot. Add one shank and brown on all sides, 3 to 4 minutes. Transfer to the slow cooker. Repeat the browning with the remaining butter and oil and the remaining shank. Lay the shanks side by side in the crock.

2. To the drippings in the pan, add the onions, carrots, and garlic and cook for 1 minute, then add to the crock over the meat. Add the shallots, celery, mushrooms, tomatoes, wine, tomato paste, and Worcestershire sauce to the crock, stirring to mix. Cover and cook on LOW for 9 to 11 hours, until the meat is very tender. During the last 45 minutes of cooking, check the consistency. If the juices are too thin for you, transfer the meat and vegetables to a serving platter using a slotted spoon, then increase the heat to HIGH and leave the cover off, letting some moisture evaporate. Season with salt.

3. Serve 1 shank per person, accompanied by the vegetables. Pour the sauce over and sprinkle with the parsley and arugula.

Osso Buco with Mushrooms

Italians make a lot of gently braised veal stews, and osso buco, a veal stew made with veal shanks, is one of the classics of their cuisine. Here is a simplified version for two, wonderfully easy in the slow cooker. It is traditionally served with Saffron Risotto (page 77). There are many variations, even an all-white version without tomato. It can also be made with red wine instead of the white. In Italy (and in America as well), it is not unusual to see a diner digging out the flavorful marrow from the inside of the bones and spreading it on crusty bread. The gremolata is a wonderful touch and really flavors the sauce, so don't skip it. If you want more flavor, add a mashed anchovy to the gremolata; it is *de rigueur* in some regions. Fresh rosemary is often added to the stew, and one beef shank can be substituted for the two veal shanks. Have the butcher saw the veal shanks crosswise into thick hunks. The meat will shrink when done so that you can see half the bone, and the meat is so creamy soft you can eat it Italian style, which is without a knife. Veal osso buco does not reheat well, so eat it the same day it is made. ○ *Serves 2*

COOKER: 3 quart
SETTING AND COOK TIME: LOW for 7 to 8 hours

½ ounce dried porcini mushrooms
2 veal shanks (about 1 pound), sawed crosswise into thick hunks (tie a piece of kitchen twine around the perimeter of the shank to hold the meat against the bone, if desired)
2 tablespoons all-purpose flour
¾ teaspoon salt
¼ teaspoon freshly ground black pepper
3 tablespoons olive oil
½ large yellow onion, finely chopped
½ medium-size carrot, finely chopped
1 stalk celery, finely chopped
½ of a 14-ounce can Italian plum tomatoes, drained and crushed
8 ounces white or brown mushrooms, thickly sliced
½ cup dry white wine
½ cup chicken broth, canned or homemade (see page 17)

GREMOLATA:
Zest of 1 lemon, cut off in strips
2 cloves garlic, peeled
¼ cup fresh Italian parsley

1. In a small bowl, soak the dried mushrooms in a few tablespoons of hot water to cover, until soft, about 10 minutes. Finely chop the mushrooms, reserving the soaking liquid.

2. Pat the veal dry with paper towels and coat with the flour, salt, and pepper. In a large skillet over medium-high heat, warm the oil until very hot. Add the veal and brown on all sides, about 5 minutes. Transfer to the slow cooker, positioning the shanks side by side if possible.

3. Add the onion, carrot, celery, tomatoes, and white mushrooms to the crock, surrounding the shanks. Add the wine, broth, porcini mushrooms, and reserved mushroom liquid. Cover and cook on LOW for 7 to 8 hours, until the veal is tender enough to cut with a fork. The veal should be cooked until falling off the bone, about 165° to 170°F on an instant-read thermometer.

4. To make the gremolata, combine the lemon zest, garlic, and parsley in a small food processor; pulse until finely chopped.

5. Transfer the shanks to a platter and cover with aluminum foil. Transfer the sauce to a small saucepan and skim off any fat. Bring to a boil and let reduce, uncovered, until it reaches the desired consistency. Add half of the gremolata and let simmer for 5 minutes. Pour the sauce over the veal and serve immediately, sprinkled with the rest of the gremolata.

Osso Buco with Fennel, Capers, and Lime

This is a Lydie Marshall recipe from *A Passion for My Provence* (Morrow, 1999), and it is just so wonderful that I had to adapt it for the slow cooker. The flavors are very different from those of classic osso buco, with licorice-like fennel, salty capers, and sweet, citrusy lime. Lydie says that this is her cooking school students' favorite dish. Use Chardonnay for the white wine; it has a distinctive character that is very different from other white wines. Have a butcher saw the veal shanks crosswise into thick hunks. ○ *Serves 2*

COOKER: 3 quart
SETTING AND COOK TIME: LOW for 7 to 8 hours;
  lime, capers, and olives added after 5½ to 6 hours

1 medium-size yellow onion, coarsely chopped

1 cup coarsely chopped fennel (about 1 bulb)

2 veal shanks (about 1 pound), sawed crosswise into thick hunks (tie a piece of kitchen twine
  around the perimeter of the shank to hold the meat against the bone, if desired)

2 tablespoons all-purpose flour

¾ teaspoon salt

¼ teaspoon freshly ground black pepper

3 tablespoons olive oil

⅔ cup Chardonnay

1 small lime, thinly sliced

2 teaspoons drained nonpareil capers

3 to 4 tablespoons coarsely chopped pitted niçoise or Gaeta olives

1. Spray the inside of the crock with nonstick cooking spray and place half of the onion and fennel in the crock.

2. Pat the veal dry with paper towels and coat with the flour, salt, and pepper. In a large skillet over medium-high heat, warm the oil until very hot. Add the veal and brown on all sides, about 5 minutes. Transfer to the slow cooker, positioning the shanks side by side if possible.

3. Add the remaining onion and fennel on top of the shanks. Add the wine. Cover and cook on LOW for 5½ to 6 hours.

4. Arrange the lime slices over the top and sprinkle with the capers and olives. Cover and cook another 1½ to 2 hours. The veal should be cooked until falling off the bone. Serve immediately.

· · Slow Cooker Tip: Transporting Slow Cookers · ·

Taking your full slow cooker to a buffet or picnic as a handy serving container? If you do not have a lid latch, wrap the lid with foil to help secure it in place. The entire cooker can be wrapped in a clean, thick towel on the car floor or in a box in the trunk, or placed in an insulated cooler (with towels wrapped around it to prevent slipping while driving) to retain heat for a long journey. Some manufacturers also sell insulated carriers and specific lid attachments for transporting their slow cookers. Upon arriving at your destination, plug in the slow cooker and set to KEEP WARM or LOW for up to 2 hours before serving.

Veal Stew with Artichokes and Potatoes

eal stew is one of the most delicious and sophisticated one-pot meals. The meat is very mild and takes on the flavors of the cooking liquid and vegetables. Here is a favorite with potatoes and artichoke hearts, which taste incredible together. If you can find fresh baby artichokes, along with freshly dug potatoes, these will make your stew all the better. ● *Serves 2*

COOKER: 1 ½ to 3 quart
SETTING AND COOK TIME: HIGH for 3 to 4 hours;
  artichoke hearts and herbs added after 2½ hours

1 pound boneless veal stew meat or veal shoulder, cut into 1½-inch chunks
2 tablespoons all-purpose flour
¼ teaspoon salt
¼ teaspoon freshly ground black pepper
2 tablespoons olive oil
2 shallots, chopped
¾ cup chicken broth, canned or homemade (see page 17)
¼ cup dry white wine
4 small new potatoes, partially peeled and cut in half
½ of a 6-ounce jar of artichoke hearts, drained, or 3 whole baby artichokes, quartered (see right)
1 tablespoon chopped fresh Italian parsley
2 teaspoons chopped fresh basil

1. Pat the veal dry with paper towels. In a plastic bag or bowl, toss the veal with the flour, salt, and pepper until evenly coated.

2. In a large skillet over medium-high heat, heat the oil until very hot. Add the veal and cook until browned on all sides, about 2 minutes. Transfer to the slow cooker. Add the shallots to the pan and cook for 1 minute or so to take the raw edge off; add to the crock. Add the broth and wine to the pan and bring to a boil, scraping up the brown bits; add to the crock along with the potatoes. Toss to combine the meat and vegetables. Cover and cook on HIGH for 2½ hours.

3. Add the artichoke hearts, parsley, and basil. Cover and cook for another ½ to 1½ hours. Serve hot.

How to Prepare Fresh Baby Artichokes

Squeeze the juice of a lemon into a large bowl of cold water; drop the squeezed-out halves in too. You will drop the artichokes into the water as you trim them, to prevent discoloring. To trim the artichokes, bend back the lower, outer petals until they snap off easily near the base. Continue to snap off the leaves until you reach the point where the leaves are half green at the top and half yellow. Using a paring knife, cut off the top cone of leaves at the crown, where the yellow color meets the green. Cut off the stem level with the base and trim any remaining green from the base. Rinse under cold water. Toss into the lemon bath and store, tightly covered, in the refrigerator until ready to use.

If you would like to freeze the artichokes, first toss them into a saucepan of boiling water with a whole clove and a splash of olive oil. Simmer, uncovered, until tender, about 30 minutes. Drain, cool, and store in zipper-top plastic bags. Thaw and cut into halves or quarters before adding them to stews and braises near the end of the cooking time.

Greek Lemon Veal Stew
with Spinach

One of my catering staff spent a summer assisting cooking classes with Rosemary Hinton Barron at Kandra Kitchen, on the Greek island of Santorini. This is one of her school recipes, adapted for the slow cooker, and it is very different from other veal stews. The lemon and spinach are a delicious combination, in both flavor and texture. The egg and lemon thickener at the end is a classic Greek touch. Serve with steamed rice and lemon wedges for squeezing all over the stew before eating. ○ *Serves 2*

COOKER: 1 ½ to 3 quart

SETTING AND COOK TIME: HIGH for 3 to 4 hours; spinach added during last 15 minutes

1 medium-size white onion, very thinly sliced

¾ teaspoon ground cumin

1 pound boneless veal stew meat or veal shoulder, cut into 1-inch chunks

2 tablespoons all-purpose flour

¼ teaspoon salt

¼ teaspoon freshly ground black pepper

2 tablespoons olive oil

¾ cup chicken broth, canned or homemade (see page 17)

Zest of ½ lemon

6 ounces fresh spinach, stems removed, leaves cut into 1-inch ribbons

1 egg yolk

2 tablespoons freshly squeezed lemon juice

2 to 4 lemon wedges for serving

1. Spray the inside of the crock with nonstick cooking spray. Place the onions in the bottom as a bed for the veal; sprinkle with the cumin.

2. Pat the veal dry with paper towels. In a plastic bag or bowl, toss the veal with the flour, salt, and pepper until evenly coated.

3. In a large skillet over medium-high heat, heat the oil until very hot. Add the veal and cook until browned on all sides, about 2 minutes. Transfer to the crock and add the broth and zest. Cover and cook on HIGH for 3 to 4 hours. At 3 hours, test the veal for tenderness. If it is tender, add the spinach, cover, and cook for 15 minutes until wilted and bright green; otherwise, cook the veal a bit longer before adding the spinach.

4. In a small bowl, beat the egg yolk with the lemon juice. Spoon off $\frac{1}{4}$ cup cooking liquid from the crock and whisk into the egg mixture. Stirring constantly, pour the egg mixture back into the stew; stir for a few minutes, until the stew liquid is thickened and heated through. Serve immediately.

Quick Accompaniments to Slow-Cooked Meals

Here is a wide range of simple but creative side dishes that cook quickly in a separate pot on the stovetop or bake in the oven while the main dish is bubbling away in the slow cooker. (And two of the dumpling recipes go right into the slow cooker, at the end of cooking!) I like to serve many of my slow-cooked meals accompanied by some sort of grain or starch. In addition to a variety of flavored rices and pilafs, there are roasted root vegetables and classic boiled potatoes, as well as

dumplings and cornbread. And since a simple mixed green salad is also a wonderful, light accompaniment, I have included a selection of my favorite salad dressings. Mix and match these dishes with your slow-cooked meals as you see fit to help lend a lot of variety to your stews, chilies, and meat and poultry dishes. These recipes are designed to provide single servings for two people, so if you want leftovers, be sure to double the recipes.

> ## •• Slow Cooker Tip: Cooking Vegetables ••
>
> Hard, heavier vegetables (such as carrots, winter squash, potatoes, turnips, and onions) take longer to cook than meat, so place them on the bottom of the cooker and set meat or poultry on top. Unskinned potatoes keep their shape better, and smaller pieces cook faster than larger chunks or whole potatoes. Cut all the different vegetables in one dish into uniform bite-size pieces so that they will cook evenly. Lighter vegetables (such as corn, peas, and summer squash) can be layered on top or added halfway through the cooking time. Unless otherwise noted, strongly flavored vegetables, like cauliflower and broccoli, are best added toward the end of cooking, so as not to flavor the entire pot.

French Pilaf

Once the French decided they liked rice, they adopted the method of sautéing the rice with butter and cooking it in chicken broth in the fashion created in the Middle East long ago. It is so easy and foolproof, yet makes a beautiful rice. If you use converted rice, use 2¼ cups chicken broth. If you have a small shallot, cook it in the butter before you add the rice; this is a delicious variation. I make enough of this rice to have leftovers, since it reheats so nicely.

o Serves 2 with leftovers

6 tablespoons (¾ stick) unsalted butter
1 cup long-grain white rice
1¾ cups chicken broth, canned or homemade (see page 17)
¼ to ½ teaspoon salt, to your taste
Freshly ground white pepper to taste

1. Melt 3 tablespoons of the butter in a small heavy saucepan over medium heat. Add the rice and stir until it begins to turn opaque, 2 to 3 minutes; do not brown. Add the broth and salt and bring to a boil.

2. Reduce the heat to the lowest setting, cover, and simmer without lifting the lid for exactly 20 minutes, at which point the rice should be cooked through and tender, and all the liquid absorbed. Remove from the heat.

3. Sprinkle pepper over the rice and stir in the remaining 3 tablespoons of butter. Let stand, covered, for 5 to 15 minutes, then serve hot.

Saffron Rice

S affron rice is so delicate and versatile. It goes with just about every stew, curry, and Italian pot roast I make. It is a good substitute for the more labor-intensive Saffron Risotto (page 77). ○ *Serves 2*

1 cup chicken broth, canned or homemade (see page 17)
½ cup long-grain white rice or basmati rice, rinsed until the water runs clear
Pinch of salt (optional)
1 tablespoon unsalted butter
Pinch of saffron threads or ⅛ teaspoon ground turmeric

1. Bring the broth to a boil in a small heavy saucepan. Add the rice, salt, butter, and saffron.

2. Reduce the heat to the lowest setting, cover tightly, and simmer until all the liquid is absorbed, 20 to 25 minutes.

3. Remove from the heat and let stand for 10 minutes, covered, then serve hot.

Basic Wild Rice

Wild rice used to be so costly that it was reserved for holidays and special-occasion meals. No more. Thanks to increased production, the price has dropped considerably over the years; now, wild rice has taken its place as one of the most satisfying starchy sides to accompany both meat and vegetables. Serve this nutty, chewy grain any day of the week with poultry and beef braises.

o *Serves 2*

⅔ cup water or chicken or vegetable broth, canned or homemade (see page 17 or 18)
¼ cup wild rice, rinsed
Pinch of salt
2 teaspoons unsalted butter

1. Bring the water to a rolling boil in a small saucepan. Add the wild rice and salt. Return to a boil, then cover and reduce the heat to the lowest setting and simmer until all the water is absorbed and the rice grains are separate, about 40 minutes.

2. Fluff with a fork, stir in the butter, and serve hot.

Seco de Quinoa

L ooking for a different side dish in place of rice? Try quinoa. Originally from South America, it is grown domestically in the United States and is a complete protein, a rarity in the family of grains. Each grain is a flat disc shape, like a tiny lentil, with a hoop-like bran layer surrounding each grain; after cooking, the bran layer looks like a half-moon-shaped crescent, a visual tip to knowing when it is cooked. Quinoa is very light and extremely digestible, with a surprising crunch. Rinse carefully before cooking, as the grains are coated with a soapy-tasting resin that acts as a natural pesticide. Unless it is rinsed thoroughly, there can be a slightly bitter aftertaste. ○ *Serves 2*

1 tablespoon olive oil
2 white boiling onions, minced
1 cup quinoa
2 cups water
¼ teaspoon salt

1. Heat the olive oil in a small heavy saucepan over medium heat. Add the onions and sauté until soft, 4 minutes.

2. Place the quinoa in a deep bowl and fill with cold water to cover. Swirl with your fingers; it will foam. Drain off through a fine-mesh strainer. Repeat until there is no foam.

3. Add the quinoa, water, and salt to the onion in the pan, stir, and bring to a boil. Reduce the heat to as low as possible, cover, and simmer without lifting the lid for exactly 20 minutes, at which point the opaque dot in the center of each grain will have disappeared and the quinoa will be translucent and fluffy, with all the water absorbed. Remove from the heat.

4. Let stand, covered, for 5 to 15 minutes, then serve hot.

Rice and Vermicelli Pilaf

From food writer Victoria Wise, author of *The Pressure Cooker Gourmet* (The Harvard Common Press, 2003), here is the original pilaf that was the inspiration for Rice-A-Roni. Other than the simple flourishes of salt, pepper, and a pat of butter at the end, this combination of rice and the thinnest spaghetti needs no extra flavoring. It is a must with all types of lamb dishes. ○ *Serves 2*

1 tablespoon plus 1 teaspoon unsalted butter
¼ cup broken-up vermicelli or fine egg noodles
½ cup long-grain white rice
1 cup water
Freshly ground black pepper to taste

1. Melt 1 tablespoon of the butter in a medium-size heavy saucepan over medium-high heat. Add the vermicelli and stir until it begins to turn golden, about 1½ minutes. Add the rice and continue to stir until well coated and translucent, about 2 minutes. Add the water and bring to a boil.

2. Reduce the heat to low, cover, and simmer without lifting the lid for 20 minutes, at which point the rice should be cooked through.

3. Sprinkle pepper over the rice and place the remaining 1 teaspoon butter on top. Cover and set aside for at least 10 minutes or for up to 30 minutes. Use two forks to fluff up the rice and mix in the pepper and butter. Serve immediately.

Bulgur Pilaf

If you have never had bulgur wheat other than in a cold salad, make this immediately; it is that good. The flavor is incredible and quite a surprise. Bulgur is a fast-cooking form of cracked wheat, and it cooks up into a nutty-flavored, satisfying starchy side to serve with your stews and chicken dishes.

○ *Serves 2*

1 tablespoon unsalted butter
½ cup bulgur wheat
1 cup water or chicken or vegetable broth, canned or homemade (see page 17 or 18)
Pinch of salt

In a small heavy saucepan, melt the butter over medium heat. Add the bulgur and stir for a few minutes to heat and coat with the hot butter. Add the water and salt and bring to a boil. Cover, reduce the heat to medium-low, and simmer until all the water is absorbed and the grains are separate, about 15 minutes. Fluff with a fork before serving.

• • Slow Cooker Tip: Liquids in the Slow Cooker • •

Always be aware of how much liquid you are using in a recipe, especially if adapting from a traditional oven or stovetop recipe. Add only the amount of liquid listed in the recipe, even if it seems like not enough, since a lot of juices from the ingredients will collect. The slow cooker does not evaporate any liquid, so less liquid is needed at the beginning. This is the condensation-cover principle of braising: As moisture rises and accumulates, condensation forms on the inside of the lid and drips back down into the food in the crock. A general rule of thumb when adapting a stovetop recipe to the slow cooker is to cut the liquid in half. You can also substitute equal amounts of different liquids, such as broth for wine, and water and bouillon cubes or granules for broth. Since slow cooking uses moist heat, you cut down on fat by using no oil or butter in most recipes. Foods also retain all their nutrients, since the closed environment does not allow vitamins to boil away.

Angel Hair Pancakes with Chives

hin noodle pancakes are a charming and special touch to add to a meal. Serve these pancakes with meat or poultry entrées. ○ *Serves 2*

4 to 6 ounces uncooked angel hair pasta
1 large egg, lightly beaten
1 heaping tablespoon minced fresh chives
A few pinches of salt
2 tablespoons unsalted butter

1. Fill a medium-size pot with water and bring it to a rolling boil. Add the pasta and cook for 1 to 1½ minutes only, lowering the heat to keep the water at a low simmer. Drain in a colander and pour into a small bowl.

2. Add the eggs, chives, and salt; mix well so all the noodles are coated with the egg.

3. Melt the butter in a medium-size skillet or on a griddle over medium heat. Divide the mixture evenly in the skillet to make 4 pancakes. Cook until brown on both sides, turning only once, about 3 minutes. Serve immediately.

Tossed tender greens are the perfect accompaniment to any slow cooker creation, whether it be a stew, a braise, or a simple chicken breast. Once you have the greens washed and stored in the refrigerator, a tossed salad is just moments away. Here are four of my favorite dressings.

Shallot Vinaigrette ● Serves 2

Try this vinaigrette with butter lettuce, mesclun, of a mix of watercress and arugula.

1 tablespoon balsamic vinegar
1 tablespoon red wine vinegar
1 small shallot, minced
5 tablespoons olive oil
Pinch of salt and a few grinds of black or white pepper

In a small bowl, whisk together all the dressing ingredients. Use immediately, or refrigerate for up to 2 days.

Spicy Cider Vinegar Dressing ● Serves 2

Any mixture of greens tastes fantastic with this dressing, as does a little crumble of nice bleu cheese or some pink grapefruit segments. It's also good with a mixture of greens, tomatoes, and avocados.

1 tablespoon cider vinegar
1 small clove garlic, minced or pressed
3 tablespoons extra-virgin olive oil
Splash of hot pepper sauce, such as Tabasco
Pinch of salt
Freshly ground black or white pepper to taste

In a small bowl, whisk together all the dressing ingredients. Use immediately, or refrigerate for up to 2 days.

Citrus Balsamic Dressing o Serves 2

Serve this over a spinach salad with red onion slivers and croutons.

1 tablespoon freshly squeezed orange juice
1 tablespoon freshly squeezed lemon juice
1 tablespoon balsamic vinegar
½ teaspoon Dijon mustard
2 tablespoons olive oil
Pinch of salt
Freshly ground black or white pepper to taste

In a small bowl, whisk together all the dressing ingredients. Use immediately, or refrigerate for up to 2 days.

Asian Vinaigrette o Serves 2

Toss this with a mixture of finely shredded carrots and cabbage, or serve it over greens of your choice.

1½ tablespoons rice wine vinegar
1 green onion (white and a bit of the green part), minced
1 teaspoon grated fresh ginger
1 teaspoon toasted sesame oil
4 tablespoons peanut oil or light olive oil
Dash of freshly squeezed lemon juice
Pinch of sugar or drop of honey
Pinch of salt

In a small bowl, whisk together all the dressing ingredients. Use immediately, or refrigerate for up to 2 days.

Oven-Roasted Roots

Roasted vegetables have a delightfully rich and intense flavor that make a satisfying side dish for your slow-cooked meals. The combination of carrots, parsnips, and yams is an excellent flavor combination all winter long. This is great with beef, pork, or poultry. ○ *Serves 2*

½ bag baby carrots, left whole
1 medium-size parsnip, thickly sliced on the diagonal
2 small sweet potatoes or Garnet yams, peeled and sliced
2 tablespoons olive oil
Salt and freshly ground black pepper to taste

1. Preheat the oven to 400°F. Line a baking sheet with aluminum foil, or use a ceramic 1-quart gratin or baking dish.

2. Combine the carrots, parsnip, and sweet potatoes in a large bowl and toss with the olive oil. Arrange the vegetables on the baking sheet or in the dish and sprinkle with salt and pepper. Bake for 25 to 30 minutes, until just tender when pierced with the tip of a knife. Serve hot.

Oven-Roasted Vegetable Spaghetti

S paghetti squash looks like pasta, but it is most emphatically a vegetable. This is for those days when you want a lighter accompaniment to your stew. It is a fabulous side dish for all manner of beef, turkey, and game stews.

o *Serves 2*

One 2-pound spaghetti squash
2 tablespoons unsalted butter, softened
2 tablespoons honey (optional)
Salt and freshly ground black pepper to taste

1. Preheat the oven to 350°F. Cut the squash in half lengthwise and scoop out the seeds. Butter the cavities, drizzle with the honey, if using, and season with salt and pepper. Place on a baking sheet and cover loosely with aluminum foil. Bake in the center of the oven until the squash is tender, about 45 minutes.

2. Remove from the oven and pull out the flesh with a fork. It will look like long strands of spaghetti. Serve hot in a mound alongside your stew.

Boiled New Potatoes with Sour Cream

I t must be my Hungarian ancestry, because I adore these potatoes as the accompaniment to all manner of meat stews and brisket. The sour cream oozes into the juices of any stew. Search out different brands of sour cream, as every one has a slightly different flavor and thickness. Use red or white potatoes, even specialty potatoes such as Yukon Gold or purple potatoes, but make sure they are of a size that allows them to be served whole. ○ *Serves 2*

1 pound red or white potatoes
2 teaspoons salt
½ to ¾ cup cold regular or low-fat sour cream

1. Place the whole potatoes in a medium-size saucepan and add water to cover by 2 inches. Bring to a boil and add the salt. Cover and cook over medium heat for 10 to 15 minutes, until tender when pierced with the tip of a knife.

2. Drain the potatoes, then return them to the hot saucepan and quickly shake them dry over direct heat. Transfer to a serving plate, or place in a bowl lined with a clean cloth napkin and cover with the napkin until ready to eat. Serve hot, with the sour cream in a bowl on the side.

Spaetzle Dumplings

S oft spaetzle dumplings, "little sparrows," are served as a side dish like noodles or rice and are delicious with all types of beef, veal, and pork stews and braises. They are a home-cooked Hungarian and German delight and are served throughout Central and Eastern Europe. If you love these, invest in the little spaetzle maker that looks like a hand grater; it is far easier than cutting them by hand. ○ *Serves 2*

1 cup all-purpose flour
½ teaspoon salt
1 large egg
3 to 4 tablespoons cold milk or water
1 tablespoon unsalted butter
Sour cream to taste

1. In a medium-size bowl, combine the flour and salt. Make a well in the middle and add the egg and milk into the center. Blend well with a wooden spoon until evenly moistened; the dough will be very thick and moist. Cover with plastic wrap and allow to rest at room temperature for 45 minutes.

2. Bring a large stockpot of salted water to a rapid boil. If shaping by hand, place the dough on a wet cutting board and rest it on the rim of the pot. Using a damp paring knife or soup spoon, cut off little irregular portions the width of a pencil and about ½ inch long at the edge of the board and let them fall into the boiling water. If using a spaetzle maker, position it over the boiling water; it will rest on the rim of the pot. Place the dough in the hopper and slide the carriage back and forth, dropping pear-shaped bits of dough into the water.

3. Simmer the spaetzle, uncovered, until they float back up to the surface, about 30 seconds. Remove with a fine-mesh strainer or slotted spoon, shake off the excess water, and place in a shallow casserole. Toss with the unsalted butter and a dab of sour cream to keep them from sticking together. Serve immediately as a side dish, or cover and refrigerate for up to 8 hours. Reheat for 12 to 15 minutes in a 350°F oven.

Slow Cooker Buttermilk Biscuit Dumplings

Dumplings are made just like a moist drop biscuit, and you can make them on top of any stew or chili that you like. If you can find a soft, unbleached flour specially for biscuits, such as White Lily, do use it; I use a combination of flours here, but you can use all all-purpose flour, if you like (make sure it is well aerated first by stirring so the cup of flour is not so dense when you measure). I find that dumplings are best eaten right after they are made; otherwise, they get soggy. For variation, add a tablespoon of chopped fresh parsley, cilantro, or basil (even a few tablespoons of grated cheese), depending on the flavors in your stew or chili. ○ *Makes 4 large or 6 small dumplings, serving 2*

½ cup all-purpose flour

⅓ cup cake flour (such as Softasilk) or whole wheat pastry flour

¼ teaspoon baking powder

¼ teaspoon baking soda

¼ teaspoon salt

2 tablespoons margarine or solid vegetable shortening

⅓ cup cold buttermilk

1. In a medium-size bowl, combine the flours, baking powder, baking soda, and salt. Cut in the margarine with a fork until it is crumbly. Stir in the buttermilk and blend until a lumpy, thick, soft dough is formed. Do not overmix.

2. Using a tablespoon, scoop out some dough and drop on top of the finished simmering stew in the crock, taking care to place the dumpling on top of solids rather than directly into the liquid, so that it will steam nicely. Repeat to make 4 or 6 dumplings. Cover and cook on HIGH for 25 to 35 minutes, until the dumplings are cooked through. Pierce the dumplings with a toothpick, bamboo skewer, or metal cake tester; it should come out clean. Serve immediately with the stew.

Slow Cooker Dumplings from a Mix

I f you have a biscuit mix, such as Bisquick, you can have dumplings ready to steam in 1-2-3. As with the Slow Cooker Buttermilk Biscuit Dumplings (opposite), these should be added in to the slow cooker at the end of the cooking time, right before serving. ○ *Makes 4 dumplings, serving 2*

1 cup biscuit mix
⅓ to ½ cup milk or water
1 tablespoon minced fresh Italian parsley or cilantro

1. Mix the ingredients together in a small bowl.

2. Using a tablespoon, scoop out one-quarter of the dough and drop on top of the simmering stew in the crock, taking care to place the dumpling on top of solids rather than directly into the liquid, so that it steams nicely. Repeat with the remaining dough. Cover and cook on HIGH for 25 to 35 minutes, until the dumplings are cooked through. Pierce the dumplings with a toothpick, bamboo skewer, or metal cake tester; it should come out clean. Serve immediately with the stew.

·· Slow Cooker Tip: Doubling Recipes ··

While all slow cooker recipes can be doubled and tripled, what seems like a simple process can easily be thrown out of balance by the liquid proportions. Plan on some experimentation to get the dish just right. To double or triple a recipe, the general rule is to multiply the liquid by one and a half times; you can add more hot liquid at the end to adjust if necessary. When multiplying recipes, make sure you have the appropriate size cooker to accommodate the increased amounts.

Olive Oil Corn Muffins

You have a choice of flavoring these muffins with vanilla extract, which is muted and complements the cornmeal, or curry powder, which makes a more distinctly savory muffin. The olive oil in place of butter is brilliant and delicious. I adapted this from *The Stanford University Healthy Heart Cookbook* (Chronicle Books, 1997), with recipes by one of my favorite cookbook writers, Helen Cassidy Page. ○ *Makes 6 muffins*

½ cup stone-ground fine cornmeal
¼ cup all-purpose flour
¼ cup whole wheat flour
2 tablespoons sugar
1½ teaspoons baking powder
Pinch of salt
⅔ cup buttermilk
1 small egg
3 tablespoons olive oil
¼ teaspoon pure vanilla extract or ½ teaspoon curry powder

1. Preheat the oven to 400°F. Grease 6 cups of a standard-size muffin tin.

2. In a medium-size bowl, combine the cornmeal, flours, sugar, baking powder, and salt. Make a well in the center and add the buttermilk, egg, oil, and vanilla or curry powder. Beat well for 1 minute by hand; the batter will be lumpy.

3. Spoon the batter into the muffin tin, filling each cup level with the top. Bake for 20 to 24 minutes, or until golden and the tops are dry and springy to the touch. A cake tester will come out clean when inserted into the center.

4. Cool in the pan for 5 minutes before transferring to cool on a rack. Serve warm. Leftovers will keep in a zipper-top plastic bag in the freezer for up to 2 months.

Hot Pepper Cornbread

 I make this sour cream cornbread in a 6-inch springform pan or pie pan. Mix a little honey into softened butter and spread that on top—you won't regret it. ◦ *Makes one 6-inch bread*

½ cup stone-ground fine cornmeal
⅓ cup all-purpose flour
1 teaspoon baking powder
Pinch of baking soda
Pinch of salt
3 tablespoons sour cream
1 tablespoon unsalted butter, melted
1 tablespoon honey
1 small egg
½ jalapeño chile, stemmed, seeded, and cut into thin rounds
⅓ cup fresh or thawed frozen corn kernels

1. Preheat the oven to 375°F. Grease a 6-inch springform pan, ceramic baking dish, or pie plate.

2. In a medium-size bowl, combine the cornmeal, flour, baking powder, baking soda, and salt. Make a well in the center and add the sour cream, butter, honey, egg, jalapeño, and corn. Beat well for 1 minute; the batter will be lumpy. Spoon the batter into the prepared pan. Bake for 20 to 25 minutes, until golden and a cake tester comes out clean when inserted into the center.

3. Transfer to a rack to cool. When cool, release and remove the sides of the pan, if necessary, and cut into small wedges to serve.

Measurement Equivalents

Please note that all conversions are approximate.

Liquid Conversions

U.S.	Metric	U.S.	Metric
1 tsp	5 ml	1 cup	240 ml
1 tbs	15 ml	1 cup + 2 tbs	275 ml
2 tbs	30 ml	1¼ cups	300 ml
3 tbs	45 ml	1⅓ cups	325 ml
¼ cup	60 ml	1½ cups	350 ml
⅓ cup	75 ml	1⅔ cups	375 ml
⅓ cup + 1 tbs	90 ml	1¾ cups	400 ml
⅓ cup + 2 tbs	100 ml	1¾ cups + 2 tbs	450 ml
½ cup	120 ml	2 cups (1 pint)	475 ml
⅔ cup	150 ml	2½ cups	600 ml
¾ cup	180 ml	3 cups	720 ml
¾ cup + 2 tbs	200 ml	4 cups (1 quart)	945 ml
			(1,000 ml is 1 liter)

Weight Conversions

U.S. / U.K.	Metric	U.S. / U.K.	Metric
½ oz	14 g	7 oz	200 g
1 oz	28 g	8 oz	227 g
1½ oz	43 g	9 oz	255 g
2 oz	57 g	10 oz	284 g
2½ oz	71 g	11 oz	312 g
3 oz	85 g	12 oz	340 g
3½ oz	100 g	13 oz	368 g
4 oz	113 g	14 oz	400 g
5 oz	142 g	15 oz	425 g
6 oz	170 g	1 lb	454 g

Oven Temperature Conversions

°F	Gas Mark	°C
250	½	120
275	1	140
300	2	150
325	3	165
350	4	180
375	5	190
400	6	200
425	7	220
450	8	230
475	9	240
500	10	260
550	Broil	290

Index

Salsa
    Chicken with Cheese, 94
    Cranberry-Orange, 135
    Mango-Ginger, 124–125
    Tomato-Olive, 194–195
    Watermelon, 152–153
Salt, adding to slow cooker, 9, 16
Sauces. *See also* Pasta sauces
    Basil, Fiorentino, 193
    Cranberries Cabernet, 134
    Cranberry Brown Gravy, 129
    Cranberry-Orange Salsa, 135
    Horseradish, 199
    Mango-Ginger Salsa, 124–125
    Pesto, 101
    Ro's Cranberry-Raspberry Conserve, 135
    store-bought, for slow cooker recipes, 12
    Tomato-Olive Salsa, 194–195
    Watermelon Salsa, 152–153
Sauerkraut
    and New Potatoes, Pork Chops with, 141
    and Pears, Country Pork Ribs with, 156
Sausage
    and Greens, Black Bean Soup with, 44
    pork, adding to slow cooker, 139
Savory, 46
Seafood, adding to slow cooker, 9
Seco de Quinoa, 216
Shallot Vinaigrette, 220
Slow cookers
    adapting traditional recipes for, 10, 218
    base, cleaning, 10–11
    cooking beans in, 64–65
    cooking method used in, 1–2
    crock insert, handling, 7, 9, 10, 76, 99
    delay timers for, 195
    doubling and tripling recipes, 227
    energy used by, 94
    filling capacity, 6, 8
    first-time use, 5–7
    food safety and, 131, 195
    foods unsuitable for, 19
    high altitude adjustments for, 14
    how they work, 2–3
    leaving unattended, setting for, 42
    leftovers, reheating, 53
    leftovers, storing, 9, 53
    lids, handling, 3, 8, 103
    liquids for, 218, 227
    pantry ingredients for, 11–14
    power outages, handling, 31
    preparing ingredients in advance, 177
    shapes of, 3–4, 49
    sizes of, 3–5
    small, manufacturers of, 4
    small, sizes of, 4–5
    temperature settings, 5, 153
    thawing frozen foods for, 69
    tips for success, 7–11
    traditional cooking time conversion chart, 10
    transporting, 3, 205
Soups. *See also* Broths; Stews; Stocks
    bean-based, adding salt to, 16
    Black Bean, with Sausage and Greens, 44
    Broccoli, Curried Cream of, 30–31
    Butternut Squash, 26
    Cauliflower, 27
    Chicken, Coconut, and Galangal, 34–35
    Chipotle Black Bean Vegetable, 45
    Fennel Potato Leek, 32
    Mushroom Barley, with Nasturtium Butter, 24–25
    Sopa de Casera with Chicken, Tofu, Avocado, and Beans, 33
    Split Pea, Winter, 39
    Split Pea, Yellow, with Cumin and Lemon, 40–41
    Tomato, Provençal, with Poached Eggs, 28–29
    Tomato Lentil, 42–43
    Turkey and Rice Congee (Jook), 36
    Turkey Minestrone, 37
    White Bean, with Bacon, 38
    Zucchini, with Oven Croutons, 22–23
Spaetzle Dumplings, 225
Spaghetti, Vegetable, Oven-Roasted, 223
Spices, adding to slow cooker, 9
Spinach
    adding to lasagna recipe, 85
    Greek Lemon Veal Stew with, 208–209
    Vegetable Polenta with Mascarpone Cheese, 72
Split Pea
    Soup, Winter, 39
    Yellow, Soup with Cumin and Lemon, 40–41
Spread, Pimiento and Garlic, 111